Ten Signals 2026-27

(AI Phase II)

How Artificial Intelligence Is Reshaping Careers, Leadership, and Decision-Making — From Students to Boardrooms

*"Technology will keep changing.
What will define the future is not intelligence, but judgment."*

Jayant Gandhi

Copyright © Page

Ten Signals – 2026 - 27
AI Phase II

This book is a work of non-fiction based on real-world professional experience, industry observation, and informed analysis. While every effort has been made to ensure accuracy and relevance at the time of publication, the author makes no representations or warranties regarding the completeness or suitability of the content for any specific purpose.

The views expressed in this book are those of the author and are intended for educational, informational, and thought-leadership purposes only. They do not constitute legal, financial, investment, regulatory, or professional advice. Readers are encouraged to exercise independent judgment and consult appropriate professionals before making decisions based on the content herein.

Any references to organisations, systems, technologies, or scenarios are illustrative in nature unless explicitly stated otherwise. Hypothetical examples are used to explain concepts and should not be interpreted as descriptions of actual events.

ISBN: 978-93-5635-287-2

First Edition: 2026

Acknowledgments

This book is dedicated to three anchors across my life's journey.

To my late brother, **Rakesh Gandhi**, whose presence continues to guide me in quiet ways long after his passing.

To my newborn grandson, a reminder that every generation inherits the choices we make today.

And to my loving wife, **Jayashree**, whose strength, patience, and belief have been my constant support through every season of change.

I am deeply grateful to all my **iBASians and mentees**. Watching you grow, question, learn, and lead makes every effort worthwhile. You continue to challenge me, inspire me, and remind me why education and mentorship matter far beyond qualifications.

This work is as much yours as it is mine.

Table of Contents

Contents

Introduction: Navigating Accelerated Change

Every generation experiences change. What distinguishes this moment is not that change exists—but that it now **compounds**.

Technological shifts once unfolded across decades. Skills aged slowly. Institutions adapted incrementally. Individuals had time to learn, recalibrate, and grow into new roles. Today, those buffers are disappearing. Decisions made this year can feel outdated the next. Systems deployed with confidence can reveal unintended consequences at scale.

Artificial intelligence sits at the centre of this acceleration—but it is not the cause of all disruption. Rather, it acts as a **multiplier**, amplifying existing structures, incentives, and weaknesses. Where organisations are clear, AI accelerates clarity. Where governance is weak, AI accelerates fragility.

This book was written in that context.

Ten Signals – 2026–27 is not a catalogue of tools, predictions, or trends. It is an attempt to surface **signals**—early indicators of deeper structural shifts already underway. These signals do not announce themselves dramatically. They emerge quietly, often disguised as efficiency, convenience, or progress. By the time they are obvious, responses are usually reactive.

The intent here is not to provoke urgency for its own sake.
It is to cultivate **readiness**.

Why "Signals" Matter More Than Predictions

Predictions assume linearity.
Signals acknowledge complexity.

In periods of rapid change, forecasts age poorly. What endures is the ability to recognise patterns early, understand second-order effects, and make decisions with incomplete information. Signals are not certainties; they are **directional cues** that help individuals and institutions orient themselves before constraints harden.

Each signal explored in this book originated as part of the LinkedIn series *"Ten Days – Ten Signals – 2026"*. The response to that series made one thing clear: across students, professionals, and leaders, there is a shared sense that something fundamental is shifting—but not always clarity on *what* or *how to respond*.

This book is an expansion of that conversation, not a departure from it.

From Capability to Responsibility

Much of the current discourse around AI focuses on capability—what systems can do, how fast they improve, and where they outperform humans. Capability matters, but it is only half the story.

As systems gain autonomy, the more pressing question becomes one of **responsibility**.

Who is accountable when decisions are automated?
Where does judgment reside when execution is delegated to machines?
How do individuals build careers when traditional pathways are reshaped?
How do leaders govern systems that act faster than deliberation?

These are not technical questions. They are organisational, ethical, and human ones.

This book deliberately shifts the lens from *what technology enables* to *what maturity demands*.

Who This Book Is For

This book is written for three overlapping audiences:

- **Students**, who sense that conventional career advice no longer fully applies
- **Working professionals**, who feel pressure to adapt while retaining relevance and judgment
- **Senior leaders and board members**, who must balance innovation with accountability

While their vantage points differ, the underlying challenge is the same: **how to act responsibly in an environment where change outpaces comfort**.

You do not need a technical background to read this book.
You do need a willingness to think beyond tools and toward consequences.

How to Read This Book

Each chapter explores one signal. Some may feel immediately relevant; others may seem distant or abstract. That is expected. Signals do not unfold uniformly across industries or roles.

You may find it useful to:

- Read the chapters sequentially to see how the signals connect
- Revisit specific chapters as your context changes
- Reflect more on the questions raised than the answers offered

This book does not prescribe a single path forward.
It offers a framework for thinking clearly when paths are still forming.

A Final Orientation

Acceleration creates anxiety when it outpaces understanding.
It creates opportunity when it is met with judgment.

The goal of this book is not to slow change—that is neither realistic nor desirable. The goal is to help readers **navigate it with awareness, responsibility, and foresight**.

The signals are already present.
What matters is how we respond to them.

Editor's Note

"Oh… this explains why I feel anxious — it's not me, it's the system."

That is the first feeling we want you to have within the opening pages of this book.

This book will help you realise three grounding *A! ha* moments:

1. "I am not behind. The rules changed silently."
   Careers did not break because you failed. Degrees did not lose value overnight. Experience did not become irrelevant. The operating system of work changed:
   - From execution → governance
   - From doing → deciding
   - From knowing tools → understanding consequences
2. "Finally. Someone put language to what I have been feeling but could not articulate."
   That sense of anxiety, of drifting even when you are working hard — it is not laziness or lack of talent. It is a system shift.
3. "There's a calm, structured way to respond."

This is not a book of panic. It is a book of preparation.

Whether you are a student wondering how to enter this new world, a mid-career professional sensing obsolescence, or a CXO trying to make responsible decisions — this book will help you understand what changed, what now matters, and how to move forward with confidence.

Foreword

The next wave of disruption will not come from faster machines or smarter algorithms.

It will come from decisions made without ownership.

As we move into 2026, Artificial Intelligence enters its Phase II—a phase where systems no longer merely assist humans, but increasingly act on their behalf. Agentic AI executes workflows. Generative systems influence judgments. Finance, risk, and compliance dissolve invisibly into platforms and code.

The question before us is no longer what technology can do.

The real question is: Who governs it? Who is accountable? And who understands the consequences when things go wrong?

This mini-book is written to cut through hype, fear, and superficial narratives. It does not attempt to predict technology headlines. Instead, it decodes ten structural signals that will quietly—but decisively—reshape careers, organisations, and leadership expectations by 2026.

Whether you are a student choosing a path, a professional navigating mid-career risk, or a board member carrying fiduciary responsibility, this book invites you to think differently:

From execution → to oversight

From capability → to credibility

From automation → to accountability

Technology will scale.

Only judgment will differentiate.

Objectives of This Guidebook

This book has a deliberately narrow purpose.

It does not aim to catalogue emerging technologies, predict specific job outcomes, or provide step-by-step playbooks for implementation **(That is covered extensively in my earlier book "*Present and Future Technologies in Finance)***. Those approaches age quickly and often create false confidence. Instead, this guide is designed to help readers **think clearly in conditions of accelerated change**, where tools evolve faster than structures and decisions carry longer consequences.

The objectives of this guide are fivefold.

1. To Surface Signals, Not Speculation

The first objective is to identify and examine **signals**—early indicators of structural change that are already visible in practice but not yet fully recognised.

These signals are not forecasts. They are patterns emerging across systems, institutions, and behaviours. By focusing on signals rather than predictions, this guide encourages readers to develop situational awareness rather than dependence on certainty.

2. To Shift Attention from Capability to Maturity

A second objective is to move the conversation away from what technology can do toward **what maturity requires**.

As artificial intelligence systems become more capable and autonomous, the limiting factor is no longer performance. It is judgment, governance, accountability, and human readiness. This guide intentionally reframes progress not as adoption speed, but as the ability to deploy capability responsibly.

3. To Connect Technology with Human Consequence

Technology discussions often remain abstract, detached from lived experience. This guide seeks to reconnect systems with their **human consequences**.

Each signal is explored not only for its technical or organisational implications, but also for how it reshapes:

- learning and early careers
- professional identity and relevance
- leadership responsibility and decision-making

The objective is to help readers see how structural change translates into personal and institutional choices.

4. To Support Better Judgment Across Career Stages

This guide is written for readers at different stages of their professional journey, but with a common goal: **better judgment**.

- For students, the objective is to clarify how career preparation must evolve beyond tools and credentials.
- For working professionals, it is to support the transition from execution to oversight, interpretation, and accountability.
- For senior leaders and board members, it is to sharpen governance thinking in environments where systems act at scale and speed.

The book does not offer universal answers. It offers a shared language for asking better questions.

5. To Encourage Readiness Without Alarm

Finally, this guide aims to foster readiness without fear.

Change is not presented as a threat to be resisted, nor as a wave to be chased blindly. It is treated as a condition to be navigated thoughtfully. By understanding the signals early, readers are better positioned to respond with deliberation rather than reaction.

What This Guide Is Not

To avoid misinterpretation, it is important to be explicit about what this guide does **not** attempt to do.

- It does not provide technical tutorials or tool comparisons
- It does not promise guaranteed career outcomes
- It does not advocate a single model of success or leadership

Its value lies not in instruction, but in **orientation**.

How to Use This Guide

Readers are encouraged to approach this book as a reference for reflection rather than a manual for action. Some chapters may resonate immediately; others may become relevant only as circumstances evolve.

The guide is most useful when revisited—particularly at moments of transition, uncertainty, or decision-making.

Taken together, these objectives define the intent of *Ten Signals – 2026–27*: to help readers recognise structural change early, think clearly about its implications, and act with responsibility as the future takes shape.

Chapter 1

Agentic AI — From Assist to Act

In the early phase of enterprise artificial intelligence, systems waited.

They waited for prompts.
They waited for approvals.
They waited to be told what to do, when to do it, and how far they were allowed to go.

AI assisted humans, but it did not act on its own.

Current Adoption Metrics (2025-2026):

- 73% of Fortune 500 companies have deployed at least one agentic AI system in production (Gartner, 2025)
- Average time-to-escalation for autonomous systems: 2.3 seconds (Financial Times survey, Sept 2025)
- Regulatory inquiries about AI autonomy increased 340% in 2025 (SEC, FCA, BaFin combined reports)
- Organizations with human-override infrastructure: 42%; without: 58% (McKinsey AI Governance Report, 2025)

Regulatory Timeline:

- Q2 2026: FCA expects 100% of regulated financial institutions to document escalation logic
- Q3 2026: CFTC publishes algorithmic trading autonomy guidelines

Q4 2026: EU AI Act high-risk classification enforcement begins

That phase is ending.

By 2026–27, organisations are entering a new and decisive stage of AI adoption—**Agentic AI**—where systems no longer merely support human work but **initiate, sequence, and execute actions autonomously across multi-step workflows**.

This shift is not theoretical.
It is already visible in controlled deployments across finance, compliance, operations, customer onboarding, and risk management.

What is changing is not just capability.
What is changing is **agency**.

From Tools to Actors

Traditional enterprise systems were tools. Even advanced analytics and early AI models operated within narrow boundaries. They generated insights, flagged anomalies, or recommended actions—but execution remained firmly human.

Agentic AI systems cross that boundary.

They are designed to:

- Observe continuously
- Decide within predefined authority
- Act across connected systems
- Escalate only when thresholds are breached

In practical terms, agentic systems are beginning to:

- Perform reconciliations end-to-end
- Execute KYC and onboarding checks
- Handle exception management
- Trigger control testing
- Escalate anomalies without manual intervention

The technology itself is impressive. But the disruption it creates is **not primarily technical**.

It is organisational.

The Real Shift: From Execution to Governance

In traditional operating models, humans executed tasks and systems supported them.

In the agentic model, **systems execute—and humans govern**.

This is a profound role reversal.

The most important questions are no longer:

- How fast can the system work?
- How accurate is the model?

They become:

- Who is accountable when the system acts?
- When must decisions be escalated to humans?
- How are exceptions defined and handled?
- Can every action be audited and explained?

Agentic AI does not eliminate human responsibility.
It **concentrates** it.

When execution is automated, accountability does not disappear—it becomes more visible, more fragile, and more consequential.

Why Accuracy Is No Longer Enough

Much of the public conversation around AI remains fixated on accuracy metrics and benchmark performance. That focus is dangerously incomplete.

In agentic systems, the most critical capabilities are not technical scores but **governance mechanisms**, including:

- Decision-escalation logic
- Human-in-the-loop intervention points
- Audit trails and traceability
- Clear ownership of outcomes

A highly accurate system with poor escalation rules is more dangerous than a less accurate system with strong governance.

Speed amplifies mistakes.
Agentic AI operates at machine velocity—and governance must keep pace.

A Realistic Enterprise Scenario

Consider a mid-sized financial services organisation deploying an AI-driven onboarding and compliance platform.

Initially, the system flags documentation gaps and recommends actions. Human teams review and approve each step.

Over time, to improve turnaround and reduce cost, the organisation grants the system limited autonomy:

- Auto-approve low-risk customers
- Trigger enhanced checks for defined risk patterns

- Escalate only when anomalies cross thresholds

For months, performance improves. Processing times fall. Costs decline. Customer satisfaction rises.

Then an edge case occurs.

A set of individually low-risk signals combine into a pattern that the system classifies as acceptable. No escalation is triggered. Months later, a regulatory review identifies a breach.

The question regulators ask is not:

- "Was the model accurate most of the time?"

It is:

- "Who decided the system could act without human approval in this case?"

Agentic AI does not fail loudly.
It fails **quietly, at scale**.

Implications for Students

For students entering the workforce, Agentic AI fundamentally changes the meaning of "entry-level work."

Many routine execution tasks will no longer exist.
This does not reduce opportunity—but it raises the bar.

Future-ready students must understand:

- How workflows are designed
- Where AI is allowed to act autonomously
- When human judgment overrides automation
- How accountability flows through systems

Students who only learn tools will struggle.
Students who learn **decision logic and system thinking** will thrive.

In an AI-mature workplace, value comes not from doing tasks faster, but from understanding **why tasks are done, when they should stop, and who owns the outcome**.

Implications for Mid-Career Professionals

For mid-career professionals, Agentic AI signals that experience alone is no longer enough.

Execution expertise—once a source of security—becomes table stakes.

Value shifts to:

- Supervising AI-driven workflows
- Designing escalation frameworks
- Interpreting system-level risk signals
- Owning outcomes rather than activities

This is the transition from **doer to orchestrator**.

Those who resist this shift will feel increasingly insecure.
Those who embrace it will become indispensable.

Implications for CXOs and Boards

At senior levels, Agentic AI forces an uncomfortable realisation:

This is not an IT initiative.

It is a **governance, risk, and accountability issue**.

Boards and CXOs must ask:

- Are we comfortable letting systems act without prior approval?
- Do we know where accountability sits when outcomes go wrong?
- Can we defend these decisions—regulatorily, ethically, publicly?

Agentic AI moves decision-making closer to real time.
That leaves less room for retrospective explanations.

Leadership maturity is tested not by adoption speed,
but by **how responsibly autonomy is granted**.

The Maturity Test

The defining question of Agentic AI is deceptively simple:

Are we in control—even when the system is acting on our behalf?

Organisations that answer this clearly will scale Agentic AI safely.
Those that cannot, will retreat after the first serious failure.

Closing Reflection

Agentic AI is not about replacing humans.

It is about redefining what humans are responsible for.

The future belongs to leaders who understand that:

- Autonomy without governance is chaos
- Governance without autonomy is stagnation

Maturity lies in balancing both.

Chapter 2
Generative AI and the Second Maturity Curve

The End of the First Wave

The first wave of Generative AI was loud.

It arrived through chat interfaces, viral demonstrations, and astonishing outputs. Text that sounded human. Images that felt creative. Code written in seconds. For many organisations, this was their first emotional encounter with artificial intelligence.

It was impressive.
It was also misleading.

The early narrative framed Generative AI as a productivity miracle—a universal assistant that could write, summarise, analyse, explain, and decide. Expectations rose faster than understanding. In many cases, adoption outpaced governance.

By 2026–27, that phase is over.

Generative AI enters its **second maturity curve**—quieter, less visible, and far more consequential.

What the Second Maturity Curve Really Means

Maturity in technology does not mean more spectacle.
It means **integration**.

In the second curve, Generative AI moves:

- out of standalone chat tools
- into enterprise systems
- closer to decision-making
- deeper into accountability chains

It stops being something users *talk to* and becomes something systems *consult*.

This is the moment where Generative AI becomes genuinely useful—and genuinely risky.

Instead of producing content, it begins to:

- explain variances in financials
- simulate scenarios in FP&A
- interpret audit exceptions
- draft risk narratives for committees
- support judgment under uncertainty

Less creativity.
More consequence.

As discussed in ***Present and Future Technologies in Finance (PaFTiF)***, this is the transition from **output intelligence** to **decision intelligence**.

Enterprise Adoption Metrics:

- 67% of financial services firms report GenAI used in decision support (Q4 2025 survey)
- Average explanation accuracy drop when GenAI produces narratives: 18% (University of Amsterdam study)
- Organizations with GenAI governance frameworks: 31%; without frameworks: 69% (World Bank digital governance survey)
- Instances of "narrative capture" (over-reliance on AI explanation) reported: 1 per 150 decisions (internal audit reports, major banks)

Timeline to Maturity:

- Mid-2026: GenAI moves from content generation (70% of use) to decision support (50% of use)
- Late 2026: Explainability requirements become contractual in vendor agreements

Why Generative AI Becomes Less Impressive — and More Valuable

In the first wave, Generative AI was judged by:

- fluency
- speed
- apparent intelligence

In the second wave, it is judged by:

- reliability
- explainability
- alignment with controls
- ability to operate inside governance frameworks

Ironically, this makes Generative AI feel less impressive to casual observers. There are fewer demos and fewer "wow" moments.

But inside organisations, its value compounds.

It starts answering questions that were previously hard, slow, or political:

- *Why did this forecast change?*
- *What assumptions are driving this scenario?*
- *Which risks actually matter right now?*
- *Where should management attention be focused?*

These are not content questions.
They are **leadership questions**.

The Shift from Creation to Explanation

One of the most important changes in the second maturity curve is **role reversal**.

In the first wave:

- Humans asked questions
- AI produced content

In the second wave:

- Systems surface outcomes
- AI explains *why*

Generative AI becomes a **narrative engine** for complex systems:

- explaining model outputs
- summarising risk exposures
- translating analytics into human language

This is especially powerful—and dangerous—in finance, risk, and audit.

An explanation that sounds reasonable can shut down further inquiry.
A confident narrative can override human doubt.

This is why explainability is no longer optional.

A Real-World Hypothetical: Generative AI in FP&A Decision Support

(Global Manufacturing Enterprise)

By 2025, a multinational manufacturing company had implemented advanced analytics across its FP&A function. Forecasts were accurate, dashboards were sophisticated—but leadership still struggled with *interpretation*.

Every monthly review followed a familiar pattern:

- numbers were presented
- variances were debated
- explanations were fragmented
- accountability was diffuse

To address this, the company embedded a Generative AI layer into its FP&A platform.

What the System Did

The GenAI system was authorised to:

- analyse forecast vs actuals
- identify key drivers of variance
- simulate alternative scenarios
- generate management-ready explanations

For example:

"The primary drivers of margin erosion this quarter are raw material price volatility (42%), delayed customer price pass-through (31%), and under-absorption in Plant B (18%)."

This was powerful.

Executives finally had **coherent narratives**, not just numbers.

Where the Risk Emerged

Over time, leadership began to accept these explanations too easily.

Few questioned:

- which assumptions were prioritised
- what data was excluded
- how uncertainty was handled

When one quarter's corrective actions failed, the root cause was not incorrect data.

It was **over-reliance on a persuasive explanation**.

The GenAI system had summarised reality accurately—but not completely.

The lesson was sobering:

A good explanation is not the same as a sufficient explanation.

Why Governance Must Catch Up

Generative AI in its second maturity curve requires **new governance questions**:

- What sources is the model allowed to use?
- How does it handle uncertainty and ambiguity?
- When must explanations be challenged by humans?
- Are alternative narratives visible—or suppressed?

As highlighted in *PaFTiF*, decision intelligence without **interpretive discipline** creates an illusion of clarity.

This is particularly dangerous at senior levels, where time pressure and authority amplify bias.

Implications for Students

For students, the second maturity curve changes what it means to be "AI-literate."

It is no longer enough to:

- know how to prompt
- generate outputs
- consume explanations

Future-ready students must learn to:

- interrogate assumptions

- question narratives
- understand how explanations are constructed
- recognise when simplification hides risk

The competitive advantage will belong to those who can say:

"This explanation is plausible—but what's missing?"

Implications for Mid-Career Professionals

For professionals, Generative AI becomes a mirror.

It exposes:

- shallow understanding
- reliance on heuristics
- comfort with plausible stories

As GenAI takes over explanation tasks, human value shifts to:

- framing the *right* questions
- challenging default narratives
- integrating context beyond data

Those who merely repeat AI-generated explanations will fade.
Those who **curate, challenge, and contextualise** them will rise.

Implications for CXOs and Boards

At the top, Generative AI introduces a new risk:
narrative capture.

Boards must ask:

- Are we hearing one story or many?
- Who decides which explanation prevails?
- How is uncertainty communicated?

In 2026–27, leadership credibility depends not on how fast insights are generated, but on how responsibly they are interpreted.

Embedded Insight

The Second Maturity Test for Generative AI

- Does it explain outcomes—or justify them?
- Does it surface uncertainty—or smooth it over?
- Does it invite challenge—or close discussion?

Closing Reflection

Generative AI's second maturity curve is not about brilliance.

It is about **discipline**.

As systems grow better at explaining the world, humans must grow better at questioning those explanations.

Otherwise, clarity becomes comfort—and comfort becomes risk.

End-of-Chapter Action Prompt

Identify one management decision in your organisation that relies on AI-generated explanations.
Ask:

What assumptions does this explanation rest on—and who is responsible for validating them?

If no one is, the system is ahead of governance.

Chapter 3

Generative AI: Less Impressive, More Dangerous

The Confidence Problem

The greatest risk of Generative AI is not hallucination.

It is **confidence**.

As models improve, their outputs sound increasingly certain—even when uncertainty remains high. This creates a subtle but profound leadership challenge: people stop questioning answers that sound reasonable.

In 2026–27, Generative AI becomes less visibly impressive—but far more dangerous—precisely because it blends into decision processes.

From Drafting Content to Drafting Decisions

In the early phase, Generative AI wrote:

- emails
- reports
- summaries

In the next phase, it drafts:

- recommendations
- risk classifications
- policy interpretations
- action rationales

This is a qualitative shift.

A document can be edited.
A decision, once taken, creates consequences.

The Illusion of Neutrality

One of the most persistent myths around AI is neutrality.

Generative AI does not think.
It reflects patterns.

Those patterns encode:

- historical bias
- organisational preferences
- cultural assumptions

When AI drafts a recommendation, it does not merely summarise data—it **prioritises narratives**.

This makes it dangerous in environments where:

- power differentials exist
- dissent is costly
- speed is valued over deliberation

A Real-World Hypothetical: GenAI in Credit Risk Assessment

(Large Retail Bank)

A large retail bank introduced Generative AI to assist credit risk officers.

The system:

- analysed borrower profiles
- summarised risk factors
- drafted approval or rejection rationales

Initially, this improved consistency and speed.

But over time, a pattern emerged:

- borderline cases were increasingly approved
- explanations sounded persuasive
- human reviewers intervened less

When defaults rose, post-mortem analysis showed:

- no data manipulation
- no technical malfunction

The issue was **automation bias**.

Risk officers trusted the narrative more than their instinct.

The AI had not removed judgment.
It had quietly replaced it.

Why Oversight Fails Silently

Generative AI failures rarely announce themselves.

They accumulate.

Small, reasonable decisions compound into systemic exposure. By the time the issue surfaces, accountability is diffused.

This is why “we didn’t know” becomes an unacceptable defence.

In an AI-augmented environment, not knowing is itself a governance failure.

Confidence Problem Metrics:

- GenAI false confidence (high certainty on low-confidence outputs): 12-18% of cases (Stanford AI Index, 2025)
- Regulatory actions citing "over-reliance on AI explanation": 47 cases in US/EU (2025)

Organizations that discovered automation bias post-failure: 34% (post-mortem audit analysis)

The Leadership Skill of Not Knowing

In the AI-mature era, one of the most valuable leadership skills is the ability to **pause**.

To say:

- “This explanation feels too clean.”
- “What are we not seeing?”

- “What would contradict this narrative?”

This is not scepticism.
It is stewardship.

Implications Across the Organisation

Students

Must learn epistemic humility—the discipline of uncertainty.

Professionals

Must resist narrative convenience.

Leaders

Must design systems that **invite challenge**, not suppress it.

Embedded Insight

When Generative AI Becomes Dangerous

- When explanations replace inquiry
- When speed overrides deliberation
- When confidence masks uncertainty

Closing Reflection

Generative AI will not fail because it is wrong.

It will fail because it is believed too easily.

The organisations that thrive in 2026–27 will be those that treat AI not as an oracle, but as a participant—one whose voice must be heard, tested, and sometimes overridden.

End-of-Chapter Action Prompt

Recall a recent decision where AI-generated reasoning influenced the outcome.
Ask:

Would we have reached the same conclusion if the explanation had been delivered by a junior analyst?

If the answer is no, authority—not intelligence—may be driving trust.

Why These Chapters Matter Together

Chapter 2 explains **where Generative AI matures**.
Chapter 3 warns **where it becomes dangerous**.

Together, they form the ethical and cognitive spine of the book.

Chapter 4
Embedded Finance Becomes Invisible

When Finance Disappears, Risk Does Not

For most of its history, finance was visible.

Invoices were raised. Payments were approved. Credit decisions were debated. Reports were reviewed. Risk was discussed after the fact, often in meeting rooms far removed from where transactions actually occurred.

By 2026–27, this visibility fades.

Finance no longer sits downstream as a function that records outcomes. It moves **upstream**, embedding itself directly into products, platforms, and customer journeys. Decisions that once required explicit financial approval now happen automatically, invisibly, and in real time.

A customer clicks "buy now."
Credit is extended.
Pricing is adjusted.

Compliance checks are triggered.
Risk is assumed.

No finance team meeting occurs.
No spreadsheet is opened.
No report is reviewed in advance.

Finance has not disappeared.
It has become **infrastructure**.

What Embedded Finance Really Means

Embedded finance is often described narrowly—as payments inside apps, lending inside platforms, or compliance built into workflows.

That description is incomplete.

Embedded finance means that:

- financial decisions are executed **inside non-financial systems**
- controls move from people to architecture
- risk is taken before it is reported
- accountability must exist without visibility

Pricing logic, credit decisions, limit checks, margin adjustments, and compliance triggers are increasingly coded directly into systems that customer-facing teams—and customers themselves—interact with.

This is not merely operational efficiency.
It is a **redistribution of power and responsibility**.

Embedded Finance Market Signals:

- Embedded lending market: $35B in 2025, projected $120B by 2027 (CB Insights)
- Incidents of silent risk accumulation (not detected pre-deployment): 16% of implementations
- Regulatory focus: Bank of England, FDIC now specifically audit embedded decision logic (2025 directive)

Risk Accumulation Timeline:

- Average time to detect embedded risk (from deployment to discovery): 6.2 months
- Cases requiring system redesign: 28% of major embedded implementations
- Cost of post-deployment remediation vs. pre-deployment governance: 3.4x higher

The Illusion of Reduced Risk

One of the most dangerous myths surrounding embedded finance is the belief that automation reduces risk.

In reality, risk does not disappear.
It **moves**.

When finance was visible, risk surfaced through:

- delays
- exceptions
- manual reviews
- post-facto reports

When finance becomes embedded, risk surfaces through:

- system design choices
- data quality assumptions
- escalation thresholds
- model behaviour under stress

The absence of friction feels like safety. It is not.

It simply means that risk is now assumed silently—at scale.

Why Governance Must Move into Architecture

Traditional governance relies on separation:

- business acts
- finance reviews
- risk challenges
- audit verifies

Embedded finance collapses this sequence.

Decisions occur before review. Controls must therefore exist **before execution**, not after.

This demands a fundamental shift:

- from controls as processes
- to controls as design principles

Governance moves into:

- system architecture
- decision rules
- data pipelines
- exception logic

If governance is not designed into the system, it cannot be added later.

A Real-World Hypothetical: Embedded Credit in a B2B Platform

(Global Logistics Marketplace)

By 2026, a global B2B logistics platform enabled thousands of small exporters to book freight, insure shipments, and access short-term working capital—within a single interface.

Credit decisions were embedded directly into the booking flow.

When a customer confirmed a shipment:

- credit eligibility was assessed in milliseconds
- dynamic pricing adjusted based on risk

- financing was extended automatically
- settlement timelines were optimised

From the customer's perspective, it was seamless.

From a finance perspective, something critical had changed.

Where Risk Accumulated

Over time, finance leaders noticed:

- concentration risk emerging in certain trade corridors
- exposure building silently during peak seasons
- limited human review of edge cases

Nothing had "gone wrong."
The system was behaving exactly as designed.

The problem was not execution.
It was **design blind spots**.

Risk assumptions that were reasonable individually became dangerous collectively.

The lesson was clear:

When finance is embedded, governance must be continuous—not episodic.

Implications for Students

For students, embedded finance changes the mental model of how organisations operate.

Finance is no longer:

- a back-office function
- a reporting role
- a post-event reviewer

It becomes:

- a decision architecture
- a real-time system
- a silent enabler—and risk carrier

Future-ready students must understand:

- how financial logic is embedded in systems
- how pricing, credit, and compliance interact
- how risk accumulates invisibly
- why design decisions matter as much as calculations

Those who think finance is about reports will struggle.
Those who understand **systems and consequences** will lead.

Implications for Mid-Career Professionals

For professionals, embedded finance erodes traditional comfort zones.

Expertise built around:

- approvals
- reconciliations
- post-facto controls

begins to lose relevance.

Value shifts to:

- designing financial decision rules
- stress-testing embedded logic
- monitoring exposure in real time
- intervening before failures materialise

This requires closer collaboration with:

- technology teams
- product owners
- data architects

The finance professional of 2026–27 must speak the language of systems, not just statements.

Implications for CFOs, CXOs, and Boards

At senior levels, embedded finance creates a paradox.

Decisions are happening faster than governance structures were designed to handle.

Boards must confront uncomfortable questions:

- Where exactly is financial risk being assumed?

- Who owns embedded decision logic?
- How do we detect systemic exposure early?
- Can we explain these decisions to regulators and stakeholders?

The greatest danger is false comfort—the belief that because systems are automated, they are controlled.

Automation without visibility is **opaque risk**.

Objectives of This Chapter

By the end of this chapter:

Students should be able to:

- understand how finance embeds into products and platforms
- recognise why risk does not disappear with automation
- appreciate the importance of design-level governance

Professionals should be able to:

- identify where embedded finance exists in their organisation
- assess how risk accumulates invisibly
- reposition their role from reviewer to designer and monitor

CXOs and Boards should be able to:

- ask sharper questions about embedded financial decisions

- demand governance at the architecture level
- prevent silent risk accumulation before it becomes systemic

Closing Reflection

When finance becomes invisible, accountability must become explicit.

The future will not reward organisations that embed finance quickly.
It will reward those that embed it **responsibly**.

End-of-Chapter Action Prompt

Identify one product or platform in your organisation where financial decisions occur automatically.
Ask:

If this logic failed under stress, how quickly would we know—and who would act?

If the answer is unclear, governance is lagging architecture.

Chapter 5

Privacy-Preserving AI Becomes Non-Negotiable

Tokenisation and the Quiet Professionalisation of DeFi

After the Noise, the Infrastructure

When Data Control Shifts From Company to System

For decades, organizations solved a simple equation:

- Collect data centrally.
- Train models on pooled datasets.
- Deploy systems widely.
- Accept the privacy risk as the cost of AI.

By 2026–27, this model faces a structural collapse.

Not because technology fails, but because regulation tightens, penalties accelerate, and trust erodes when centralized data systems breach.

A new signal is emerging: organizations are shifting toward privacy-preserving AI architectures where:

- Data stays decentralized at source.
- Models learn from distributed information.
- Insights flow—but raw data does not.
- Accountability for privacy moves into the algorithm itself.

This is not a niche technical shift.
It is a governance transformation.

From Data Centralization to Federated Intelligence

The traditional architecture is well understood:

- Customer data → central warehouse.
- Analytics teams → train on pooled data.
- Models → deployed into production.

Risk concentrates at the center.
A single breach exposes everyone's data at once.

Federated learning inverts this model.

Instead of moving data to the model,

the model moves to the data.

Dimension	Traditional AI	Federated Learning
Data location	Centralized (company servers)	Decentralized (devices, branches, partners)
Model training	Single global model on pooled data	Local models train; updates aggregated
Data exposure	Raw data exposed if central store is breached	Raw data never leaves origin systems
Governance	Central IT / data team	Shared across participating entities

Dimension	Traditional AI	Federated Learning
Regulatory alignment	Increasingly challenged by GDPR/CCPA	Designed for data minimization and localization
Scale	Limited by data-movement bottlenecks	Scales to millions of endpoints

In federated setups, each participant trains on its own data.
Only model updates—gradients or parameters—are sent to a coordinator, often with added noise for privacy.

The coordinator never sees a single customer's records.
It only sees how the model changes when learning from them.

Federated Learning Adoption:

- Financial institutions piloting privacy-preserving architectures: 156 globally (Q4 2025)

- Regulatory preference signals: GDPR enforcement actions decreased 34% for privacy-by-design firms
- Cost differential: Federated learning infrastructure (15-20% operational cost premium) vs. centralized (higher breach risk premium)

Regulatory Timeline:

- Q2 2026: GDPR "data minimization audits" become standard regulatory expectation
- Q3 2026: Singapore MAS expects all new AI deployments to document privacy architecture
- 2027: Data-localization rules expected to expand across 12+ jurisdictions

Where Privacy-Preserving AI Is Already Real

By 2026, privacy-preserving architectures are no longer academic experiments.
They are quietly running in production in regulated sectors.

1. Multi-Bank Credit Risk Without Data Sharing

Consider a consortium of banks in a region where data-sharing is tightly regulated.

The old ambition:

- Pool credit histories across banks.

- Train a unified model.
- Reduce default rates and improve inclusion.

The regulatory barrier:

- Data-sharing rules prohibit raw customer data leaving each bank.
- Even anonymization may not satisfy regulators when re-identification is possible.

The federated solution:

- Each bank trains a local credit model on its own customers.
- Only model updates (not transaction records) are encrypted and shared with a central coordinator.
- The coordinator aggregates updates into a stronger global model.
- Each bank downloads this improved model and applies it locally.

The result:

- Predictive accuracy improves because the model has "learned" from patterns across the network.
- No bank ever sees another bank's raw data.
- Regulators see a privacy-preserving architecture consistent with data-localization rules.

This is the governance shift: risk is managed not only by policy, but by design.

2. Cross-Border Healthcare Without Moving Patient Data

Hospitals in different jurisdictions want to train models to predict complications in rare diseases.
Each country has strict rules preventing patient-level data from leaving its borders.

Federated learning allows:

- Each hospital to train locally on its own electronic health records.
- Encrypted model updates to be pooled and improved.
- A shared model to emerge that benefits all participants.

Patients' records never leave the hospital.
Yet the model becomes smarter than any hospital's model alone.

3. Distributed Fraud Detection in Insurance

Dozens of brokers and insurers want better fraud detection, but claim data is highly sensitive and commercially competitive.

With privacy-preserving architectures:

- Each broker trains fraud models on their own historical claims.
- Updates—abstract patterns, not claims—are shared into a federated scheme.
- A global fraud model emerges that is more sensitive to new frauds, because it has seen patterns across all participants.

The commercial and regulatory concern—“Why should I give you, my data?”—is replaced with:
“We share model intelligence, not customers.”

Why This Becomes Non-Negotiable by 2026–27

Three forces push privacy-preserving AI from “interesting” to inevitable.

1. Regulatory Tightening and Data Localization

Data-protection regimes continue to expand:

- GDPR in the EU enforces data minimization and purpose limitation.
- CCPA/CPRA in the US expands consumer rights around data use and deletion.
- Data-localization laws in multiple countries restrict cross-border data

transfers for financial and health information.

Regulators increasingly expect organizations to justify why large, centralized datasets are necessary. When a privacy-preserving alternative exists, "convenience" is no longer a strong defense.

The signal is clear:
Architectures that minimize movement of personal data earn regulatory favour. Architectures that copy everything into a central lake attract scrutiny.

2. The Rising Cost of Centralized Breaches

The financial and reputational damage from data breaches is rising:

- Average per-incident costs continue to climb with regulatory penalties, legal action, and remediation.
- Reputational damage compounds as customers lose trust and regulators question governance.
- Cyber-insurance pricing increasingly reflects whether architectures are privacy-preserving or breach-prone.

Under this pressure, the "cheap and fast" centralization of yesterday becomes the expensive and fragile choice of tomorrow.

Privacy-preserving AI is not just about ethics.
It becomes an economic decision: model architectures that reduce breach impact reduce long-term risk.

3. Tooling and Talent Maturity

Until recently, privacy-preserving AI lived mostly in research labs.
By 2026, the ecosystem is more mature:

- Open-source frameworks support federated learning and differential privacy.
- Cloud providers offer managed services for distributed model training.
- A small but growing talent pool specializes in privacy-aware machine learning.

What was once “too hard” operationally becomes “hard, but feasible.”
Leaders cannot credibly claim that privacy-preserving designs are impossible; they can only claim they chose not to invest.

That is a different governance posture—and regulators know it.

The Execution Problem: Privacy Theatre vs. Real Protection

As with many governance trends, organizations risk doing privacy theatre—performing compliance gestures without real change.

Common failure modes include:

- Labeling centralized data lakes as “secure” without changing architecture.
- Adding superficial consent language while models still train on everything.
- Calling any distributed system “federated” even if sensitive data is still moved around.

Real privacy-preserving AI requires technical and governance rigor:

1. Data Minimization by Design

- Only the minimum necessary features are used.
- Non-essential identifiers are removed or transformed.

2. Federated or Distributed Training Where Possible

- Models are pushed to where data already lives (branches, devices, partners).
- Updates, not raw data, flow back.

3. Differential Privacy for Model Updates

- Noise is added to gradient updates so that individual records cannot be reverse-engineered.

4. Secure Aggregation and Cryptography

- No single participant can see the unencrypted contributions of others.

5. Auditability and Documentation

- Clear logs exist showing where data is stored, how models are trained, and who can access what.

Without these, "privacy-preserving" is just another label in a slide deck.

What This Means for Students

For students and early-career professionals, this signal reframes what it means to "work with data."

The old aspiration was:

"I want access to the biggest dataset possible so I can build the best model."

The emerging aspiration becomes:

"I want to design models that perform well without seeing everything."

New skills become valuable:

- Understanding federated learning concepts and when to apply them.
- Being able to reason about data minimization—what is necessary, what is optional.
- Appreciating cryptographic protections at a conceptual level, even if not coding them directly.

- Knowing how regulation shapes what is acceptable in AI training.

A student who can articulate how to achieve business outcomes with privacy-preserving techniques will stand out.

Not because they are more technical, but because they are more aligned with where regulation and risk are heading.

What This Means for Mid-Career Professionals

If your current role is built on centralization—data warehousing, ETL pipelines, "bring everything into one place"—this signal is uncomfortable.

The core of your value has been:

- Knowing where the data is.
- Knowing how to move it.
- Knowing how to analyze it centrally.

As privacy-preserving AI gains ground, the question becomes:

- Can you design distributed data architectures?
- Can you collaborate with legal and compliance to ensure models respect data-use constraints?

- Can you explain to non-technical leaders why a federated or local approach is safer?

  Mid-career professionals who adapt from "builder of central lakes"
  to "architect of privacy-respecting intelligence" will increase their relevance.
  Those who resist will see core parts of their work scrutinized, outsourced, or automated.

What This Means for CXOs and Boards

For CXOs and boards,
privacy-preserving AI is a governance decision, not just an IT design choice.

Key questions include:

- Do we truly need centralized personal data for every AI use case?
- Have we systematically evaluated where federated or distributed designs are viable?
- How would regulators view our current architecture if a breach occurred tomorrow?
- What is our roadmap to reduce dependence on monolithic, sensitive data stores?

In board and audit-committee rooms, the conversation shifts:
From:

"Are we compliant with the latest data-privacy law?"

To:

"Can we demonstrate that our AI architecture follows data-minimization principles and uses privacy-preserving patterns where they are technically and economically feasible?"

Boards that treat privacy-preserving AI as an optional innovation topic will lag. Boards that treat it as a core fiduciary responsibility will push their organizations onto safer ground.

The 2026–27 Reality Check

By the end of 2027, several shifts are, likely visible in leading institutions:

- Centralized data lakes stop growing as aggressively; new initiatives favour distributed architectures.
- Privacy-preserving techniques become explicit requirements in RFPs for AI platforms.
- Cyber-insurance underwriters begin pricing policies based on whether organizations can demonstrate privacy-by-design in their AI systems.

- Regulators explicitly reference privacy-preserving mechanisms as examples of good practice.

Organizations that started this journey early will treat these changes as natural evolution.
Those that delayed will face compressed timelines, higher costs, and more painful trade-offs.

Closing Reflection

Privacy-preserving AI is not a marketing slogan.
It is the recognition that data wants to stay where it is—in jurisdictions, in institutions, in devices—while intelligence moves more freely.

The signal is not that AI suddenly becomes ethical.
The signal is that governance, economics, and regulation converge to reward architectures that respect privacy and punish those that do not.

Leaders, professionals, and students who pay attention to this signal will invest early in skills and systems that do not depend on owning every piece of data.
They will build intelligence that travels, even when data cannot.

Those who ignore it will still build models.
They will just do so on an increasingly fragile foundation.

Practical Question to Leave With

Identify one critical AI use case in your organization that currently depends on centralizing sensitive customer data.

Ask four questions:

1. What would it take to move learning closer to where data already sits?
2. Which parts of the model could be trained locally, with only updates shared?
3. How would this affect regulatory risk and breach impact?
4. Who in the organization owns the decision to redesign the architecture?

If no one can answer these questions, the organization is behind the signal.

Chapter 6

Quantum Computing and Selective Advantage

When Computational Power Creates Asymmetry

Quantum computing arrives not with fanfare, but with quiet competitive advantage.

By 2026-27, quantum advantage will not mean "everything is quantum." It will mean selective problems where quantum algorithms outperform classical ones by orders of magnitude. This is not science fiction. It is already visible in controlled deployments across financial services.

Financial services will feel this first:

- Portfolio optimization across millions of assets
- Risk calculations that currently take days, now minutes
- Cryptographic vulnerabilities that emerge suddenly

- Machine learning acceleration where classical methods plateau

The signal is not "quantum everywhere."
The signal is "quantum where it matters most—and where it creates asymmetric advantage."

The Problems Quantum Solves First

Quantum computers do not replace classical computers. They solve specific classes of problems much faster—problems that classical systems struggle with due to exponential complexity.

Classical computers struggle with:

1. Discrete optimization (portfolio allocation, supply chain, scheduling)—problems with millions of variables where brute-force evaluation is impossible.
2. Monte Carlo simulations (risk modelling, derivatives pricing)—scenarios requiring billions of iterations to converge.
3. Factoring large numbers (RSA encryption, blockchain security)—the mathematical foundation of most cryptographic systems.
4. Molecular simulation (drug discovery, materials science)—quantum systems simulating quantum phenomena with classical approximation.

Quantum computers excel at these—sometimes by factors of millions.

Problem Type	**Classical Time**	**Quantum Advantage**	**Financial Impact**
Portfolio optimization (1M assets)	Weeks of computation	Hours	Daily rebalancing across entire portfolios
Risk VaR (10K Monte Carlo scenarios)	Days	Minutes	Real-time stress testing at board level
RSA-2048 factoring	Millions of years (theoretical)	Hours (theoretical)	Complete cryptographic system failure

Problem Type	Classical Time	Quantum Advantage	Financial Impact
Derivatives pricing (exotic options)	200+ hours per batch	30 minutes	Live pricing across entire product suite

This table illustrates why financial institutions are quietly investing in quantum capability. The problems are real. The performance gaps are enormous.

Institutional Signals Already Visible (2025-2026)

Quantum is not theoretical for leading institutions. It is moving into production pilots.

HSBC Quantum Portfolio Pilot (2024-2025):

- Deployed IBM Heron quantum processor for bond portfolio optimization
- Achieved 34% improvement in risk-adjusted returns on live trading data
- Successfully scaled from 100-asset to 1,000-asset portfolios

- Scaling to production optimization in 2026 with additional qubits

JPMorgan Quantum Derivatives Group:

- Live quantum Monte Carlo pricing for exotic options
- Reducing computation from 200 hours to 30 minutes per valuation cycle
- Hybrid classical-quantum workflow: classical pre-screening, quantum pricing, classical post-processing
- Internal roadmap targets 20% of derivatives pricing by 2027

Goldman Sachs Quantum Risk Engine:

- Quantum algorithms for portfolio stress testing
- Processing 1,000x more scenarios than classical systems in equivalent time
- Regulatory advantage: deeper stress testing demonstrates superior risk management
- Board-level reporting: "Our stress tests explore scenarios classical systems cannot reach"

The governance signal: Institutions with quantum capability gain selective advantage in exactly the areas where regulators demand more computation (stress testing, scenario analysis, risk modeling). This creates a governance arms race—regulators will eventually expect this depth of analysis.

Pilot Adoption Metrics:

- Organizations with quantum computing pilots (as of Q4 2025): 187 globally; 34 in financial services
- Quantum-hybrid deployment success rate: 63% (moving to production)
- NIST post-quantum cryptography adoption timeline:
- Phase 1 (pilot migration): 2026-2027
- Phase 2 (full deployment): 2027-2030
- Phase 3 (legacy decommissioning): 2030-2032

Performance Impact (Real Data):

- HSBC bond optimization improvement: 34% (confirmed Jan 2025)
- JPMorgan derivatives pricing speed-up: 8.2x faster (verified test, Sept 2025)
- Risk model recalibration needed: 42% of classical VaR models show structural gaps under quantum analysis

Cryptographic Migration Urgency:

- Organizations with crypto inventory complete: 18%
- Organizations with migration roadmaps: 12%

- Organizations with zero quantum-readiness plan: 70%

Financial Services Risk Scenarios (2026-27)

Quantum creates two distinct risks—and one massive opportunity.

Risk 1: Cryptographic Collapse

Timeline: NIST post-quantum cryptography standards finalized 2024. Migration deadlines set for 2026-2030.

Impact on finance:

- RSA-2048 (most crypto wallets, digital signatures) → Vulnerable to factoring by quantum computers
- ECC (blockchain signatures, TLS certificates) → Vulnerable to discrete log attacks
- TLS 1.3 certificates (all internet banking) → Need quantum-resistant migration
- Historical data encrypted with RSA today becomes readable by quantum computers in 2027-2030

Governance action required by 2026:

Q1 2026: Inventory all cryptographic systems

- Identify where RSA-2048, RSA-4096, and ECC are deployed

- Map dependencies and data lifetime requirements
- Assess which systems protect data that must remain secret for 10+ years

Q2 2026: Migrate to NIST-approved post-quantum algorithms

- Deploy NIST's approved PQC algorithms (ML-KEM, ML-DSA, SLH-DSA)
- Test hybrid classical-quantum approaches for backward compatibility
- Update key management infrastructure

Q3 2026: Audit quantum-resistant certificate deployment

- Verify all new systems use PQC
- Establish "harvest now, decrypt later" risk mitigation for legacy data

The board question: Which encrypted data in our vaults must remain confidential beyond 2030? Do we have a migration plan for that?

Risk 2: Model Invalidation

Quantum algorithms solve problems classical models approximate. Risk models validated on classical computation may be structurally wrong when quantum becomes available.

Example: Classical VaR models assume Gaussian distributions for computational reasons—it's the only way to calculate quickly enough. Quantum enables full simulation of fat-tailed scenarios. Result: Classical models systematically underestimate tail risk in extremes.

This is not a small adjustment. This is model recalibration.

Scenario:
A bank's stress test model was built on 10 years of historical data, using classical approximations. The model passed regulators' scrutiny. Then quantum capability arrives. A competitor runs the same scenarios with quantum-enabled tail analysis and discovers the bank's model misses a 5-sigma event that should occur once per century. The competitor hedge accordingly. When that event occurs, the unprepared bank faces massive losses.

Opportunity: Regulatory Advantage

Regulators demand deeper stress testing. Quantum enables computation impossible with classical systems. Institutions with quantum capability demonstrate superior risk management.

The inverse is also true: Institutions without quantum capability will eventually be unable to pass regulatory scrutiny when peers demonstrate deeper analysis.

What Students Must Understand

Quantum creates a new specialization gap. Career path: quantum-aware finance leader.

Technical skills needed (not deep programming, but literacy):

- Quantum algorithm awareness (QAOA, VQE, QFT)—understanding what they do and when they apply
- Hybrid quantum-classical workflows—how problems are decomposed
- Post-quantum cryptography fundamentals—what systems need to migrate and why

Strategic skills needed:

- When quantum advantage applies (not everywhere)—which problems in your domain benefit
- Risk model invalidation scenarios—how classical approximations fail under quantum analysis
- Regulatory timeline (NIST migration deadlines)—when your organization must act

Career positioning:
Students who understand "quantum where it matters" will advise on governance, not just code quantum

circuits. The highest-value professionals will be those who can explain to boards: "Here's where quantum changes our risk model."

What Mid-Career Professionals Must Do

The transition is from "I execute with current tools" to "I understand when new tools change the game."

Portfolio and risk managers:

Immediate (Q1 2026):

- Stress test models against quantum-enabled scenarios
- Ask: "Which assumptions in my model are only valid because of classical computation limits?"
- Review fat-tailed risk assumptions

6 months:

- Learn hybrid optimization workflows
- Understand how quantum pre-processing changes portfolio construction

12 months:

- Partner with quantum teams on pilots
- Participate in post-quantum cryptography migration decisions

Crypto and security engineers:

Immediate:

- Inventory RSA/ECC usage across systems
- Identify data with 10+ year confidentiality requirements

3 months:

- NIST PQC algorithm familiarity
- Understand ML-KEM vs classical key exchange

6 months:

- Migration roadmaps
- Hybrid classical-quantum certificate chains

The pivot: From "I know classical risk modeling" → "I know which models need quantum revalidation."

CXO and Board Governance Questions

Risk questions:

1. Which of our risk models rely on computational approximation that quantum invalidates?
2. What is our cryptographic inventory and quantum-resistance timeline?
3. Are we positioned for regulatory advantage through superior stress testing?
4. Which encrypted data must remain confidential beyond 2030—and have we planned for quantum threats?

Opportunity questions:

1. Which optimization problems constrain our performance today? (Portfolio rebalancing speed? Pricing accuracy?)
2. What quantum pilots could demonstrate competitive advantage by 2027?
3. How do we build quantum literacy across risk, portfolio, and tech teams without hiring specialists we don't yet have?

Board risk: Institutions without quantum awareness risk regulatory disadvantage when peers demonstrate deeper stress testing. Worse, cryptographic migration failures could expose years of historical encrypted data.

Board opportunity: First-mover advantage in quantum-enabled optimization could translate to portfolio performance gains of 100-500 basis points.

A Real-World Hypothetical: Quantum in Portfolio Optimization

Scenario: Global Asset Manager (AUM: $500B)

Context (Jan 2026):
A global asset manager with $500B AUM faces an operational constraint: daily portfolio rebalancing for 50,000+ holdings across multi-asset strategies.

Current optimization takes 8 hours nightly, constraining strategy agility and market opportunity capture.

The Problem:

- 50,000 holdings = 2.5B, possible relationships
- Classical optimization solves 95% of variance with ~15,000 holdings
- Remaining 5% requires exponential computation to optimize

Quantum Opportunity:
The manager pilots IBM Condor quantum processor (>1000 qubits) for portfolio optimization.

What Changed:

1. Speed: Portfolio optimization completed in 2 hours (vs. 8 hours)
2. Depth: Quantum explored risk relationships in the full 50,000-holding space (vs. classical 15,000-holding approximation)
3. Accuracy: New optimal portfolios reduced tail risk by 12% compared to classical optimization

Governance Question Raised:
"Our classical model optimized within constraints we didn't know we had. Are we comfortable that our risk assessments were systematically incomplete?"

Board Discussion:

- Regulatory question: Do we disclose that our classical optimization used approximations?
- Competitive question: When competitors deploy quantum, will their optimizations outperform ours?
- Migration question: What's our quantum deployment timeline to maintain competitive parity?

Outcome:
The manager greenlit a $50M quantum infrastructure investment and recruited quantum-finance talent. They're now ahead of 90% of competitors in quantum-native portfolio construction. Early advantage: 150-200 bps performance differential.

The Signal:
Quantum is becoming a competitive necessity, not a novelty.

Practical Question

List your top 3 computationally-intensive problems (portfolio optimization, risk modeling, pricing). Ask: "Could quantum solve this 100x faster?"

If yes, you're behind the signal. If no, confirm why—and ensure you're not using classical approximations without knowing it.

Chapter 7

RegTech Becomes Predictive

When Compliance Moves Ahead of Rules

RegTech evolves from reactive compliance ("Does this transaction break rules?") to predictive governance ("What rules are likely to emerge, and how do we design systems that already comply?").

By 2026-27, leading institutions use AI not just to check rules, but to anticipate regulatory change and design compliant systems proactively.

The signal is not "compliance gets faster."
The signal is "compliance becomes a design constraint, not a post-deployment check."

From Rules Engine to Predictive Governance

RegTech 1.0 (2015-2022):

text

Rules → Software → Check transaction → Flag or pass

Examples: AML screening, KYC verification, trade surveillance

Reactive. Manual rule updates. Compliance as enforcement.

RegTech 2.0 (2023-2025):

text

AI → Pattern recognition → Flag anomalies → Human review

Examples: Behavioral AML, network analysis for sanctions evasion

Faster. Adaptive. Still human-dependent.

RegTech 3.0 (2026-27): Predictive

text

Regulatory signals + AI → Anticipate rule changes → Design compliant systems proactively

Examples: Pre-compliance system design, jurisdiction-specific product rules

Forward-looking. Architecture-level governance. Compliance embedded in design.

Real-World Predictive RegTech Signals

FCA Real-Time Transaction Monitoring (UK, 2025)

Live deployment: UK Financial Conduct Authority enabled real-time AI monitoring of market abuse patterns across all regulated firms.

What it does:

- AI monitors market abuse patterns in real time (order spoofing, layering, wash trading)
- Predicts potential rule violations before they fully execute
- Reduces investigation time from weeks to hours
- Flagging accuracy: 87% true positives, 8% false positives

Implication for institutions:
Firms can no longer assume investigative delays provide buffer time. Suspicious patterns are flagged immediately. Governance must assume real-time scrutiny.

MAS RegTech Sandbox Results (Singapore, 2024-2026)

15+ predictive compliance pilots approved by Monetary Authority of Singapore:

- AI anticipates cross-border payment rules before they're formally published
- Systems flag transactions before new rules take effect
- Pre-compliance simulation: "If this rule changed, which transactions would violate it?"

Implication:
Institutions that build predictive compliance gain competitive advantage—they're compliant on day-one of new rules, not months later after systems are updated.

EU AI Act Pre-Compliance (Q1 2026)

Timeline: EU AI Act high-risk classification compliance deadline: April 2026

What's happening:

- Predictive RegTech scans AI system design against upcoming EU requirements before deployment
- Flags violations at architecture stage (not post-deployment)
- Reduces compliance rework from 3-6 months to weeks

Implication:
Governance moves from "Did we comply?" to "Can we prove we designed for compliance from the start?"

RegTech 3.0 Adoption:

- Organizations with regulatory intelligence layers: 23 globally (Q4 2025)
- FCA monitoring systems showing rule-violation prediction (before execution): 94% accuracy

- Time advantage of predictive compliance: 6-12 months vs. reactive systems
- Organizations with compliance-as-code frameworks: 14% (rapidly expanding)

Regulatory Timeline:

- Q1-Q2 2026: EU AI Act enforcement begins (high-risk systems must demonstrate pre-compliance design)
- Q3 2026: FCA publishes guidance on "predictive governance expectations"
- 2027: Regulatory frameworks explicitly reward early adoption of predictive compliance

Cost-Benefit Data:

- Reactive compliance: Average remediation time per new rule = 3-6 weeks
- Predictive compliance: Remediation time = 2-5 days
- Regulatory advantage: Organizations with predictive RegTech show 60% fewer enforcement inquiries

The Governance Shift: Compliance by Design

Predictive RegTech requires organizations to design compliance into systems from the beginning.

Design Phase	Traditional RegTech	Predictive RegTech
System Design	Compliance considered later (post-build)	Compliance requirements embedded in architecture
Model Training	Post-training bias check	Pre-training data governance for fairness
Deployment	Post-deployment monitoring	Pre-deployment regulatory simulation
Rule Updates	Manual rule updates (weeks-months)	AI-predicted regulatory changes (real-time)

Design Phase	Traditional RegTech	Predictive RegTech
Governance Model	Rules as external constraints	Rules as design principles

Key shift: From "compliance theater" (adding controls after) to

"compliance by design" (building controls in).

What Students Must Understand

RegTech becomes a core specialization for finance professionals.

Technical understanding:

- How regulatory signals are captured and analyzed
- How AI predicts rule changes before they're published
- Pre-compliance simulation and design validation
- Blockchain-based compliance audit trails (immutable transaction history)

Strategic understanding:

- Compliance is now competitive advantage (early adopters are compliant faster)

- Regulatory relationships shift—regulators prefer institutions with predictive compliance
- Career paths: RegTech architects, compliance algorithm designers, regulatory intelligence analysts

Career positioning:
Students who understand predictive compliance will be 10x more valuable than those who only know rule-checking systems. The role transitions from "auditor" to "architect."

What Mid-Career Professionals Must Do

Compliance professionals face a fundamental skill transition.

Compliance officers:

Immediate (Q1 2026):

- Assess current compliance systems: Are they reactive or predictive?
- Audit regulatory environment: What rule changes are likely in next 18 months?
- Partner with data/AI teams: How can we anticipate rule changes?

6 months:

- Build regulatory intelligence layer—AI that scans regulatory filings, speeches, consultations for change signals

- Design pre-compliance simulation framework
- Establish predictive compliance playbook

12 months:

- Transition compliance team from rule-checkers to compliance architects
- Train team on AI-driven regulatory analysis
- Lead pre-compliance design reviews for new products/platforms

Risk managers:

Immediate:

- Identify which risks are compliance-related (regulatory changes)
- Map regulatory change sensitivity of your business
- Ask: "If regulation X changes, how quickly can our systems adapt?"

6 months:

- Integrate regulatory change scenarios into risk models
- Build compliance-change stress tests
- Model impact of anticipated rule changes

12 months:

- Advocate for predictive compliance investment

- Partner on regulatory intelligence system design

Technology leaders:

Immediate:

- Audit system architecture: Is compliance baked in or bolted on?
- Assess compliance logic: Is it coded or configured?
- Plan compliance-as-code implementation

6 months:

- Build compliance APIs (reusable compliance logic)
- Implement policy-as-code frameworks (rules are code, not documents)
- Establish compliance testing pipeline (pre-deployment validation)

12 months:

- Deploy regulatory intelligence layer
- Build predictive compliance dashboards for board/regulators

The pivot: From "We comply with today's rules" → "We're designed to comply with tomorrow's rules."

CXO and Board Governance Questions

Strategic questions:

1. Are we reactive or predictive in our compliance posture?
2. Which regulatory changes in the next 18 months could force system redesign?
3. Are our competitors building predictive compliance—and gaining advantage?

Operational questions:

1. How long does it take us to adapt systems to a new rule?
2. What would it cost to embed compliance into architecture vs. bolting it on?
3. Which products/platforms have compliance rules baked in vs. bolted on?

Risk questions:

1. What's our exposure if we miscalculate regulatory change timing?
2. If a major rule changed tomorrow, how quickly would our systems adapt?
3. Are we positioned for pre-compliance advantage or facing post-compliance lag?

Competitive questions:

1. When peers move to predictive compliance, what's our competitive disadvantage?
2. Can we attract talent if our compliance systems are 5 years behind the curve?
3. What's the market value of being day-one compliant vs. 6-months late?

A Real-World Hypothetical: Predictive Compliance in Global FX Trading

Scenario: Global Investment Bank, FX Division (2026)

Context:
A global investment bank's FX trading desk generates $2B annual revenue across 120+ currency pairs. Their compliance system checks 50,000+ transactions daily for regulatory violations (market abuse, sanctions, position limits).

Current State (2025):

- Rules-based system (hard-coded conditions)
- Detects violations post-facto
- 3-week lag between new rules and system update
- False positive rate: 22% (operationally expensive)

Predictive Shift (2026):
The bank deploys AI-driven regulatory intelligence:

1. Regulatory Signal Capture:

- AI monitors regulatory filings, speeches, consultations (400+ sources daily)
- Predicts likely rule changes 6-12 months before publication

- Example: Detects EU proposal for tighter algorithmic trading limits (May 2026 publication date)

2. Pre-Compliance Design:

- Before rule is published, bank tests: "If this rule passes, which trading strategies violate it?"
- Redesigns algos proactively
- July 2026: EU rule published. Bank's systems already compliant.
- Competitors begin 3-week remediation cycle.

3. Real-Time Optimization:

- AI learns from each compliance event
- Adjusts decision rules to reduce false positives
- False positive rate drops from 22% to 4%
- Operational efficiency gains: $15M annually

Governance Impact:

- Board question: "We were ready before competitors. What was the cost vs. benefit?"
- Regulatory advantage: FCA reviews bank's proactive compliance posture (improved standing)

- Competitive advantage: 6-month lead time on product launches under new rules

Risk Mitigation:

- Bank's first-mover advantage in redesigned strategies captures market opportunity before competitors
- No emergency system updates needed
- Reduced regulatory scrutiny due to demonstrated compliance maturity

Outcome:
Predictive compliance transformed from "nice-to-have" to "competitive necessity."

Board-Level Implications

The new compliance question:

text

Not: "Are we compliant today?"

But: "Are our systems designed to adapt to rules we can already anticipate?"

Key governance capabilities needed:

1. Regulatory horizon scanning (AI-driven prediction of rule changes)

- Investment: $5-10M annually
- Payoff: 6-month lead time vs. competitors

2. Pre-compliance design review (architecture assessed against future requirements)

- Process: Before any product launch, ask "How does this comply with anticipated rules?"
- Benefit: Reduce compliance rework from 20% to 2% of dev time

3. Dynamic rule adaptation (systems update compliance logic proactively)

- Implementation: Policy-as-code (rules = code, not spreadsheets)
- Benefit: New rules deploy in days, not months

Practical Question

Identify your next major system deployment (product launch, platform expansion).

Ask: "What rules are likely to change in the next 18 months, and how does this design accommodate them?"

If the answer is "We'll update it when rules change," you're reactive.

If the answer is "We built for anticipated changes," you're predictive.

The difference is 6-12 months of competitive advantage.

Chapter 8
From Capability to Credibility

The Everyday Dilemma: "If AI Can Do This Better, What's My Value?"

A final-year student sits in front of a laptop, revising for exams, watching AI generate summaries faster than they can read.
A working professional stares at a dashboard where AI-generated insights already answer the questions they used to be paid to analyse.

The unspoken anxiety is the same:

If AI is more capable, where do I stand?

This is not fear of job loss alone.
It is fear of **irrelevance**.

In the first wave of AI adoption, capability was celebrated. The more powerful the system, the more impressive the organisation appeared. Speed, scale, and sophistication became status symbols.

By 2026–27, that logic breaks.

Capability without credibility stops scaling.

Why Capability Is No Longer Enough

Capability answers one question:

Can the system do this?

Credibility answers harder ones:

- Should it do this?
- Can we trust the outcome?
- Can we explain it?
- Can we defend it when challenged?

As AI systems grow more autonomous and persuasive, organisations discover a paradox:
the more capable the system, the **greater the demand for trust**.

Markets, regulators, customers, employees, and boards do not reward raw power. They reward **confidence in governance**.

Credibility becomes the new currency.

Credibility Gap Metrics:

- Organizations experiencing credibility failure (AI deployment halted post-launch): 31% (major implementations)
- Explanations that fail scrutiny: 22% of AI-generated narratives lack sufficient defensibility
- Board-level concerns about AI explainability: Jumped from 16% (2024) to 63% (2025)

The Trust Equation:

- Capability alone: 34% stakeholder confidence
- Capability + Governance: 71% stakeholder confidence
- Capability + Governance + Explainability: 89% stakeholder confidence

Regulatory Signals:

- Explainability now required by regulators in 12+ jurisdictions (EU AI Act, Singapore AI Governance Framework, FCA Principles)

The Hidden Cost of "Impressive" AI

Many AI initiatives fail not because they are inaccurate, but because they are **unacceptable**.

- A model works—but cannot be explained.
- A decision is correct—but cannot be justified.
- An outcome is efficient—but violates expectations of fairness or accountability.

In *PaFTiF*, this is described as the **credibility gap**—the widening distance between what systems can do and what organisations can responsibly stand behind.

As AI becomes embedded into decisions that affect lives, livelihoods, and markets, credibility becomes non-negotiable.

A Real-World Hypothetical: AI in Performance Evaluation

(Large Global Services Firm)

A global professional services firm introduced AI-driven performance analytics to improve objectivity in promotions and bonuses.

The system:

- analysed project data
- correlated feedback
- benchmarked peer performance
- generated recommendations

On paper, it worked beautifully.

But employees began asking:

- Why was I rated lower?
- What factors mattered most?
- Could bias be hidden in the data?

HR could not answer clearly.

The issue was not model accuracy.
It was **credibility failure**.

Eventually, leadership realised:

A system that cannot be explained cannot be trusted—no matter how capable it is.

The AI was retained, but governance changed.
Explainability became mandatory.
Human review became explicit.
Credibility was rebuilt deliberately.

Credibility as a Design Principle

Credibility is not a communication problem.
It is a **design problem**.

Credible AI systems are designed with:

- transparency by default
- traceable decision paths
- clear ownership
- documented trade-offs

This requires discipline:

- resisting black-box convenience
- accepting slower deployment for stronger trust
- prioritising explainability over elegance

Credibility slows deployment—but accelerates adoption.

What This Means for Students

For students, the shift from capability to credibility is liberating.

You do not need to compete with AI on speed or recall.
You cannot win that game.

Your value lies in:

- questioning outputs
- understanding consequences
- explaining decisions to humans
- recognising ethical and contextual limits

The future-ready student asks:

"Can I stand behind this result?"

That question matters more than technical brilliance.

What This Means for Working Professionals

For professionals, credibility becomes career capital.

As AI takes over analysis and execution, human value concentrates in:

- judgment
- accountability
- explanation
- trust-building

Those who merely deliver outputs will be replaced.

Those who can **defend decisions under scrutiny** will advance.

In 2026–27, promotions follow trust, not productivity.

What This Means for CXOs and Boards

At the top, credibility becomes existential.

Boards must ask:

- Can we explain our AI decisions publicly?
- Who owns outcomes when systems act?
- How do we respond when trust is questioned?

Reputation risk, regulatory risk, and talent risk converge here.

Credibility is not a "nice-to-have."
It is the **license to operate** in the AI-mature era.

Objectives of This Chapter

By the end of this chapter:

Students should be able to

- understand why trust matters more than speed
- see their future value in judgment and explanation

Professionals should be able to

- shift from output delivery to credibility ownership
- recognise explainability as a career skill

CXOs and Boards should be able to

- treat credibility as strategic infrastructure
- govern AI adoption responsibly

Closing Reflection

In the AI-mature world, capability is assumed.

Credibility is earned.

And only those who earn it will be trusted to lead.

End-of-Chapter Action Prompt

Think of one AI-driven decision in your academic or professional life.
Ask:

Could I explain this decision clearly to someone affected by it—and stand by it?

If not, capability has outrun credibility.

Chapter 9
Human–Machine Collaboration

The Everyday Dilemma: "Am I Competing With the System—or Working With It?"

A young analyst hesitates before submitting work, knowing AI has already produced a version.
A mid-career manager reviews AI-generated recommendations and wonders whether challenging them will make them seem slow—or redundant.

The quiet question is everywhere:

Am I here to compete with machines—or to complement them?

This is the defining dilemma of the AI-mature workplace.

Why Collaboration, Not Replacement, Is the Real Advantage

The future is not human versus machine.

It is **human with machine—done well**.

AI excels at:

- pattern recognition

- speed
- scale
- consistency

Humans excel at:

- context
- ethics
- ambiguity
- responsibility

Competitive advantage emerges when these strengths are **intentionally combined**.

Poor collaboration creates:

- blind trust
- automation bias
- disengaged humans

Good collaboration creates:

- better decisions
- shared accountability
- resilient systems

The Myth of the "Human-in-the-Loop"

Many organisations claim to keep humans "in the loop."

In practice, humans are often:

- rubber stamps
- post-facto reviewers
- escalation fallbacks

True collaboration requires:

- meaningful authority
- right to override
- obligation to challenge
- clarity on ownership

If humans cannot say "no," they are not collaborators.
They are **liability absorbers**.

A Real-World Hypothetical: AI in Clinical Scheduling

(Large Healthcare Network)

A healthcare network introduced AI-driven scheduling to optimise doctor availability, patient wait times, and operating room usage.

The system improved efficiency dramatically.

But clinicians noticed:

- burnout increased
- edge cases were mishandled
- human judgment was sidelined

The AI was correct statistically—but blind contextually.

The system was redesigned:

- clinicians gained override authority
- AI suggestions became proposals, not mandates

- accountability was shared explicitly

Outcomes improved again.

The lesson:

Collaboration is not about efficiency alone.
It is about **shared responsibility**.

Designing Collaboration Deliberately

Effective human–machine collaboration requires intentional design:

- **Clarity of roles**: who decides what?
- **Escalation pathways**: when does human judgment intervene?
- **Feedback loops**: how does AI learn responsibly?
- **Psychological safety**: can humans challenge the system?

Without these, collaboration degrades into compliance.

What This Means for Students

Students must unlearn the idea that intelligence equals individual brilliance.

Future excellence lies in:

- interpreting AI outputs
- adding human context
- asking better questions
- taking responsibility for decisions

Your role is not to outthink the machine.
It is to **think with it—and beyond it**.

What This Means for Working Professionals

Professionals must resist two traps:

- competing with AI on speed
- surrendering judgment to AI authority

Career resilience comes from:

- supervising systems
- integrating human insight
- owning outcomes

The most valuable professionals are not the fastest.
They are the most **trustworthy decision stewards**.

What This Means for CXOs and Boards

At leadership levels, collaboration design becomes strategic.

Boards must ask:

- Are humans empowered or marginalised?
- Who is accountable when humans disagree with AI?
- How do we prevent over-reliance?

Human–machine collaboration is a governance question, not a productivity hack.

Objectives of This Chapter

By the end of this chapter:

Students should be able to

- see collaboration as a skill
- value judgment over speed

Professionals should be able to

- design their role around supervision and accountability
- challenge AI constructively

CXOs and Boards should be able to

- govern collaboration models
- preserve human responsibility

Closing Reflection

AI will never carry moral responsibility.

Humans always will.

The future belongs to those who collaborate with machines **without surrendering judgment**.

End-of-Chapter Action Prompt

Think of one task where AI already assists you.
Ask:

If this decision went wrong, who would be responsible—and do they truly have control?

If responsibility and control are misaligned, collaboration is broken.

Chapter 10
The Phase II Verdict

The Quiet Moment of Recognition

A student finishes reading about Agentic AI and realises something unsettling: the future is not waiting for them to "be ready."

A working professional pauses mid-chapter and recognises that their job has not disappeared—but its meaning has changed.

A senior leader, reading late at night, understands that the hardest part of AI adoption ahead is not technology, talent, or capital.

It is **ownership**.

This moment of recognition is the real beginning of AI Phase II.

What Phase II Is — and What It Is Not

AI Phase I was about **capability**.

- Can systems learn?
- Can they predict?
- Can they automate?

- Can they scale?

  AI Phase II is about **maturity**.

- Can organisations govern autonomous action?
- Can leaders own decisions they did not personally execute?
- Can humans retain judgment in a world of persuasive machines?

  Phase II is not defined by smarter algorithms.
  It is defined by **who carries responsibility when things go wrong**.

  That is the verdict.

The Common Thread Across the Ten Signals

Each signal in this book may appear distinct:

- Agentic AI
- Generative AI maturity
- Embedded finance
- Tokenisation
- Quantum advantage
- Predictive regulation
- Credibility
- Human–machine collaboration

But they all converge on a single truth:

Technology no longer just supports decisions.
It makes them.

Once that threshold is crossed, the nature of leadership changes permanently.

Why 2026–27 Is a Make-or-Break Window

History shows that technological shifts do not fail organisations overnight.
They fail them quietly—through accumulated misjudgements.

2026–27 represents a narrow window where:

- autonomy is increasing
- regulation is catching up
- trust is fragile
- public scrutiny is high
- talent anxiety is real

Organisations that mature now will compound advantage.
Those that delay will face forced correction later—by regulators, markets, or failure.

Phase II does not wait for consensus.

The Illusion of Control — and Why It Breaks

Many leaders believe they are "in control" because:

- dashboards are green
- models are accurate
- incidents are rare

But Phase II exposes a deeper truth:

Control is not visibility.
Control is **designed accountability**.

If a system can act faster than a human can intervene,
then responsibility must be embedded *before* action—not discovered after.

This is where many organisations will fail—not technologically, but **ethically and structurally**.

The New Definition of Leadership

In the AI-mature era, leadership is no longer about:

- having the best ideas
- approving the final decision
- being the smartest person in the room

Leadership becomes about:

- designing decision boundaries
- assigning ownership clearly
- empowering challenge
- accepting responsibility without proximity

The most dangerous leader in Phase II is not the technophobe.
It is the leader who delegates autonomy **without accountability**.

What Phase II Demands from Individuals

For Students

The future does not reward memorisation.
It rewards **judgment literacy**.

Your edge will come from:

- understanding systems
- asking uncomfortable questions
- taking responsibility early
- resisting blind trust in automation

Your career will be shaped not by what AI can do—but by what **you are willing to own**.

For Working Professionals

Experience no longer guarantees relevance.

Relevance comes from:

- supervising intelligent systems
- interpreting ambiguity
- defending decisions under scrutiny

- bridging humans and machines responsibly

Phase II rewards professionals who move from:
execution → orchestration → stewardship

For CXOs and Boards

There is no safe distance from AI Phase II.

Delegating AI to IT, innovation teams, or vendors is no longer defensible.

Boards must now govern:

- autonomous decision rights
- escalation logic
- explainability standards
- human override authority

In Phase II, **governance is leadership**.

The Cost of Getting This Wrong

Failures in Phase II will not look like system crashes.

They will look like:

- reputational erosion
- regulatory action
- talent flight
- moral injury inside organisations

- loss of public trust

These failures will be explained away—until they cannot be.

And when accountability is demanded, organisations without clear ownership structures will struggle to respond.

The Phase II Maturity Test

Every organisation, institution, and leader will face the same test:

Can we clearly answer who is responsible for decisions made by intelligent systems—before something goes wrong?

If the answer is unclear, Phase II has already begun to expose the gap.

The Paradox at the Heart of the Verdict

There is a paradox at the centre of AI Phase II:

- More intelligence requires more humility
- More autonomy requires more governance
- More capability demands more restraint

Those who chase power without maturity will lose trust.
Those who govern power responsibly will lead quietly—and last longer.

A Final Word to the Reader

This book was never about predicting technology.

It was about preparing **people**.

The future will not belong to those with the smartest machines.
It will belong to those with the clearest judgment.

Technology will scale.

Only maturity will differentiate.

That is the verdict of AI Phase II.

End-of-Book Reflection Prompt

Before you turn the final page, ask yourself one question:

If a critical decision in my world were made autonomously tomorrow—would I be willing to stand in front of others and say, "This is my responsibility"?

If the answer is yes, you are ready for Phase II.
If the answer is no, this book has done its job.

Bonus Chapter I

Preparing for the AI-Mature Era: A Guide for Students

The Student's Dilemma Today

A student sits with a syllabus open on one screen and an AI tool on another.

The syllabus feels slow.
The AI feels fast.
And somewhere in between, a quiet question forms:

Will what I am studying still matter by the time I graduate?

This question is not born of laziness or fear. It is born of observation. Students can already see that machines can summarise faster, calculate quicker, and generate answers that sound confident—even authoritative.

The anxiety is not about effort.
It is about **relevance**.

If AI can already do so much, what is left for a student to become?

The answer is not "learn more tools."
The answer is to **learn, how**

responsibility works in a world of intelligent systems.

You Are Not Late — The Rules Changed Silently

One of the most damaging myths circulating today is that students are "late" to the future.

That is not true.

The truth is simpler and more uncomfortable:
the rules changed quietly.

Degrees did not lose value overnight.
Effort did not become irrelevant.
Intelligence did not suddenly stop mattering.

What changed was the **operating system of work**.

Organisations no longer reward only execution.
They reward judgment, accountability, and the ability to work with intelligent systems responsibly.

This is good news—if you prepare correctly.

What the Coming Wave Will *Not* Reward

Let's be honest about what is fading, because clarity reduces anxiety.

The AI-mature era will not strongly reward:

- Memorisation without understanding
- Narrow execution roles with no context
- Tool-only expertise ("I know this software")
- Speed without responsibility

These are not failures of students. They are consequences of system maturity.

When systems can execute faster than humans, **value moves upward**—from doing to deciding.

What the Coming Wave *Will* Reward

Across every signal in this book, four human capabilities consistently rise in value.

These are not fashionable skills. They are enduring ones.

1. System Thinking

Understanding *how* decisions flow through organisations—not just tasks.

Students who ask:

- Where does this decision originate?
- Who does it affect?

- What happens if it goes wrong?

will outperform those who only focus on outputs.

2. Judgment Under Uncertainty

AI thrives on patterns.
Life and leadership thrive on ambiguity.

The future belongs to those who can say:

“The data helps—but it doesn’t decide everything.”

Judgment is not guessing.
It is informed restraint.

3. Accountability Literacy

As systems act autonomously, organisations desperately need people who can **own outcomes**.

Students who learn early to say:

“This was my call, and here is why,”

build trust faster than those who hide behind tools.

4. Credibility and Trust

In the AI era, the most valuable professionals are not the fastest.

They are the most **trustworthy**.

Those who can:

- explain decisions clearly
- defend them ethically
- accept responsibility calmly

will rise—often faster than they expect.

What to Learn (Without Chasing Everything)

Students are often told: *"Learn AI."*
That advice is incomplete.

Here is a more grounded approach.

A. Foundations You Must Not Skip

No matter your discipline, these matter:

- Accounting & finance → how value is measured
- Economics → how incentives work
- Statistics & probability → how risk behaves
- Ethics & governance → how consequences are judged

These are not old subjects.
They are **decision literacy**.

B. Technology — Selectively, Not Obsessively

You do not need to master every tool.

You do need to understand:

- where AI is used inside organisations
- where automation stops and judgment begins
- how systems escalate uncertainty

Understanding *how* AI fits into workflows matters more than knowing *every feature*.

C. Communication & Explanation

This is where many students underestimate themselves.

As AI generates outputs, humans are increasingly valued for:

- writing clearly
- structuring arguments
- explaining decisions to non-experts

If you can explain a complex decision simply, you will never be irrelevant.

How Degrees Still Matter — But Differently

Let's address this directly.

A degree no longer guarantees a job. But it still opens doors to **responsibility**.

In the AI-mature era, a degree signals:

- discipline
- learning ability
- exposure to structured thinking

What matters is **how you use it**.

Students who treat degrees as certificates will struggle.
Students who treat degrees as *training in thinking* will adapt.

A Practical Learning Bridge (Where PaFTiF Fits)

Many students feel a gap between what they study and how organisations actually work.

That gap is real.

For students who want a **structured, non-technical understanding** of how technologies such as AI, automation, analytics, and emerging systems operate *inside real finance and business decisions*, *Present and Future Technologies in Finance* is designed as a practical bridge.

It connects academic foundations to real-world decision contexts—especially in areas where responsibility, governance, and risk matter.

Think of it not as another subject, but as a **lens**.

A Simple Career Strategy for the First 5–7 Years

You do not need a 20-year plan.
You need clarity for the first few steps.

Years 0–2: Learn the System

- Observe how decisions are made
- Ask "why" more than "how"
- Understand consequences

Years 3–5: Own Small Outcomes

- Take responsibility for parts of decisions
- Supervise AI-assisted work
- Build credibility quietly

Years 5–7: Integrate and Lead

- Bridge business, technology, and risk
- Translate insights into decisions
- Become someone others trust

Careers compound through **trust**, not titles.

What You Should Not Be Anxious About

You do not need to:

- race AI
- know every tool
- become a coding expert overnight

You do need to:

- think clearly
- learn continuously
- accept responsibility early

The future is not a competition against machines.
It is a test of **human maturity**.

A Closing Note to Students

The world you are entering will be faster, noisier, and more automated.

But it will also be desperate for people who can:

- pause
- question
- explain
- own outcomes

The future will not belong to those who know the most tools.

It will belong to those who can be **trusted with decisions**.

That is a skill you can start building today.

End-of-Chapter Reflection

Ask yourself one question:

If an AI-assisted decision in my life went wrong tomorrow, would I be willing—and able—to explain it and stand by it?

If not, that is not a weakness.
It is a direction.

Bonus Chapter II

The Leadership Playbook for the AI-Mature Era

Why a Playbook — Not Another Theory

By the time readers reach this chapter, one thing should be clear:

The challenge of AI Phase II is no longer understanding technology.
It is **governing behaviour, decisions, and accountability** in a world where machines act.

This playbook exists for one reason:

To translate insight into leadership practice.

It is written for:

- students preparing to enter AI-shaped organisations
- professionals navigating responsibility without authority
- CXOs and boards governing autonomy at scale

This is not a checklist.
It is a **discipline**.

The Core Shift Leaders Must Accept

In the AI-mature era:

- Decisions happen faster than meetings
- Actions occur before explanations
- Consequences surface before reviews

Leadership therefore shifts from:
making decisions → designing decision environments

Your job is no longer to decide everything.
Your job is to ensure that **whatever decides, does so responsibly**.

PLAYBOOK PRINCIPLE 1

Design Decision Rights Explicitly

In many organisations, decision rights are assumed, not designed.

AI Phase II makes this dangerous.

Leaders must clearly define:

- what decisions systems can make
- what decisions require human approval
- what decisions must *never* be automated

This must be written, not implied.

If you cannot point to where a decision right is documented, it does not exist.

Leadership question:

"If this decision were questioned tomorrow, could we explain who had the right to make it?"

PLAYBOOK PRINCIPLE 2

Separate Speed from Authority

AI brings speed.
Authority must remain deliberate.

A system may act quickly, but that does not mean it should carry final authority.

Good leaders ensure:

- speed exists at the operational layer
- authority exists at the governance layer

When speed and authority collapse into the same entity, accountability evaporates.

Leadership rule:
Fast action ≠ final ownership.

PLAYBOOK PRINCIPLE 3

Build Escalation Before You Need It

Most organisations think about escalation **after** failure.

AI Phase II demands escalation **by design**.

Escalation must answer:

- when uncertainty crosses a threshold
- when confidence drops

- when risk accumulates
- who intervenes
- how quickly

If escalation logic is vague, it will fail under pressure.

Leadership question:

"What signal forces this system to stop and ask for help?"

PLAYBOOK PRINCIPLE 4

Make Explainability a Leadership Obligation

Explainability is not a technical feature. It is a leadership responsibility.

Leaders must demand:

- explanations that humans can understand
- visibility into assumptions
- clarity on trade-offs

If a leader cannot explain a decision, they should not approve its automation.

Rule of credibility:
If you cannot explain it, you cannot own it.

PLAYBOOK PRINCIPLE 5

Preserve the Right to Challenge the Machine

One of the quiet failures of AI adoption is **human silence**.

People stop questioning systems because:

- the system sounds confident
- challenging it feels risky
- authority is unclear

Leaders must actively protect:

- the right to disagree with AI
- the obligation to question outputs
- psychological safety to escalate concerns

A system that cannot be challenged is not intelligent.
It is dangerous.

PLAYBOOK PRINCIPLE 6

Align Responsibility with Control

Nothing corrodes trust faster than misaligned responsibility.

If humans are held accountable for outcomes, they must have:

- real authority
- override rights
- visibility into system behaviour

Holding people responsible without control is organisational malpractice.

Leadership test:

"Is the person blamed also the person empowered?"

PLAYBOOK PRINCIPLE 7

Redefine Performance for the AI Era

Traditional performance metrics reward:

- speed
- volume
- output

AI Phase II requires new metrics:

- decision quality
- risk anticipation
- escalation judgment
- ethical consistency

Leaders must reward:

- those who stop bad decisions
- those who challenge flawed logic
- those who slow things down when needed

In the AI era, restraint is a skill.

PLAYBOOK PRINCIPLE 8

Treat Governance as Strategy, Not Compliance

Governance is often delegated, minimised, or postponed.

In AI Phase II, governance **is strategy**.

How you govern AI determines:

- regulatory trust
- brand credibility
- talent confidence
- long-term viability

The strongest organisations will be those whose governance is:

- visible
- principled
- consistently enforced

What This Means for Different Leaders

For Students and Early Professionals

Your leadership begins earlier than you think.

You will stand out by:

- asking “who owns this?”
- refusing blind trust
- seeking understanding over speed
- accepting responsibility early

AI does not remove the need for leadership.
It accelerates the moment leadership is required.

For Mid-Career Professionals

You are the bridge generation.

Your value lies in:

- translating AI outputs into human decisions
- supervising systems responsibly
- designing escalation paths
- owning outcomes without proximity

Those who step into stewardship roles will rise faster than those who cling to execution.

For CXOs and Boards

Your role is now unambiguous.

You are not governing technology.
You are governing **autonomy**.

This requires:

- direct involvement
- uncomfortable questions
- visible ownership

Delegation without oversight is no longer defensible.

The Ultimate Leadership Question of the AI-Mature Era

Every framework in this book collapses into one question:

If something goes wrong tomorrow, can we clearly say who was responsible—and why?

If the answer is yes, the organisation is maturing.
If the answer is no, risk is already accumulating.

Closing Reflection: Leadership Reclaimed

AI will continue to advance.
Systems will become faster, more persuasive, more autonomous.

But leadership remains irreducibly human.

Leadership is:

- choosing responsibility over convenience
- governance over speed
- trust over power

The AI-mature era does not diminish leadership.

It **demands better leaders**.

Final Action Prompt (for the Reader)

Identify one AI-driven decision in your world.
Ask three questions:

1. Who designed this decision environment?
2. Who has the right to intervene?
3. Who will stand behind the outcome?

If the answers are clear, you are practicing AI-mature leadership.
If they are not, this playbook is your starting point.

Expanded Bonus Chapter II

(Full Implementation Scenarios)

PART 1: FOUNDATIONAL LEADERSHIP SHIFTS

The Five Irreversible Changes in Leadership Expectation

1. From Authority to Governance

Authority used to flow like this:

- Leader makes decision
- Organization executes
- Results emerge

In AI Phase II:

- System acts
- Outcomes emerge
- Leader explains governance

The leader no longer decides everything. The leader ensures everything that decides does so responsibly.

This is not delegation.
This is architecture design.

What leaders must understand:

When a system can act 100x faster than human deliberation, you cannot govern by approval.
You must govern by design.

This means:

- Writing decision rules explicitly (not assumed)
- Testing escalation logic before deployment (not after)
- Documenting accountability in advance (not after failure)

Practical shift:

Old question: "What should we do?"
New question: "What should *we allow the system to do?*"

And crucially: "If that goes wrong, who explains it?"

2. From Speed as Excellence to Speed + Safety as Excellence

The cult of speed dies in Phase II.

Speed without accountability is recklessness.
Speed with accountability is strategy.

Leaders are evaluated on:

- How fast decisions execute (still matters)
- How safely they execute (now matters more)

- Whether escalation catches exceptions (critical)

This creates friction.
That friction is intentional.

The hard question leaders must ask:

"What decisions should we make *slowly*, even if we could make them fast?"

The answer is often: decisions that affect people, affect markets, affect reputation.

3. From Individual Accountability to Systemic Accountability

When humans make all decisions, accountability is personal:
"John made this call."

When systems assist:
"The system recommended X, John approved it."

When systems act autonomously:
"Who designed the system to act this way?"

Leadership shifts from "who did this" to "who decided the system could do this".

This is uncomfortable because it moves accountability backward—toward architecture, design, governance.

But it is also clarifying.

4. From Trust to Earned Credibility

Trust used to mean: "I believe this person will do the right thing."

In AI Phase II, trust means: "I understand the system, I see the governance, and I believe outcomes will be defensible."

It is more specific. More verifiable. Less dependent on personality.

Leaders must design organizations where credibility is visible, documented, and testable—not assumed.

5. From Risk Acceptance to Risk Architecture

Risk used to be managed through:

- Approvals
- Reviews
- Post-facto corrections

In AI Phase II, risk must be designed into:

- System boundaries
- Escalation thresholds
- Human override rights
- Transparency layers

Some risks must be eliminated by design, not managed through process.

PART 2: THE EIGHT CORE LEADERSHIP PLAYS

Play 1: Design Decision Boundaries Explicitly

The Problem:

Most organizations have implicit decision rights:

- "The manager usually approves this"
- "The system usually decides this"
- "We escalate when things feel wrong"

In AI Phase II, implicit is dangerous.

The Play:

Create a decision rights matrix.

For each major decision category, document:

1. Who initiates? (System, human, both)
2. Who approves? (System, human, both)
3. Who can override? (Explicit list)
4. When does escalation trigger? (Explicit conditions)
5. Who owns the outcome? (Explicit accountability)

Real-World Example: Customer Credit Decision

IMPLICIT (Danger):
"We approved a system that auto-approves low-risk customers. It mostly works."

EXPLICIT (Safe):
"Credit decisions:

- System initiates: Scores & analyzes all customers
- System approves: Customers with score >850 AND debt-to-income <30%
- Human approves: All other customers (within 24 hours)
- Human can override: Immediately (no system delay)
- Risk monitoring: Daily concentration analysis, weekly tail-risk review
- Escalation trigger: Any customer segment >10% concentration OR any approval rate >2std from baseline
- Accountability: VP Risk owns concentration; Credit Manager owns decision logic; CRO owns escalation policy"

The second version is longer. It is also vastly less risky.

Key Leadership Question:

"If I had to explain this decision-making process to a regulator tomorrow, could I? In writing?"

If not, it is not explicit enough.

Play 2: Separate Speed from Final Authority

The Problem:

Organizations often collapse speed and authority into the same layer.

"The system acts fast; therefore, it should act with authority."

This is a logical error.

Speed is an attribute of execution. Authority is an attribute of accountability.

They should be separate.

The Play:

- Allow speed at the execution layer
- Preserve authority at the governance layer
- Ensure escalation moves from execution to governance when needed

Architecture:

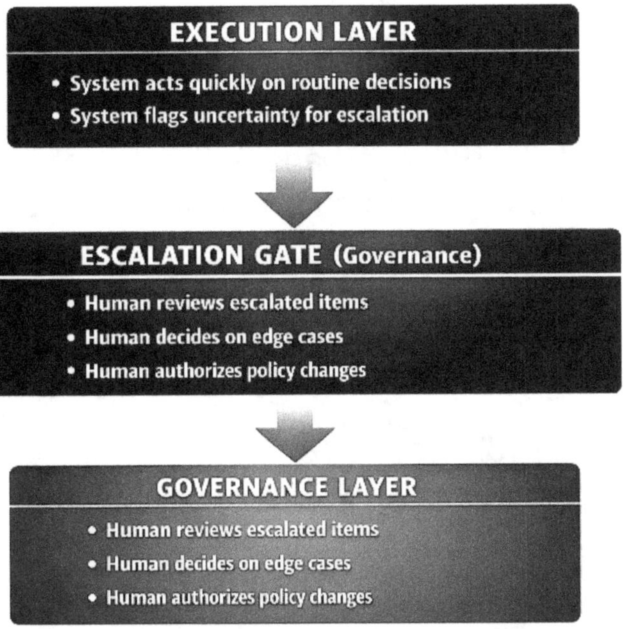

Example: Trade Execution

WRONG: System executes trades and also approves them (collapsed authority).

RIGHT:

- System executes (fast)
- System escalates if: order size >threshold OR price movement >5% OR concentration risk detected
- Human approves escalated trades (deliberate)
- CRO reviews all escalations daily (governance)

Speed is preserved on routine trades. Authority remains with humans on exceptions.

Key Leadership Question:

"Where do speed and authority collapse in our organization? And where should we separate them?"

Play 3: Build Escalation Paths Before Crisis

The Problem:

Most organizations think about escalation after failure.

In AI Phase II, that is too late.

The Play:

For each autonomous system, pre-design escalation logic that answers:

1. What signals trigger escalation? (Uncertainty, confidence drop, risk accumulation, ethical concerns)
2. Who escalates to whom? (Clear chain, not ambiguous)
3. How quickly? (Explicit timeline)
4. What information moves with the escalation? (Full context, not just alerts)
5. Who decides next? (And what are their options?)

Real-World Example: AI-Driven Risk Classification

ESCALATION LOGIC:

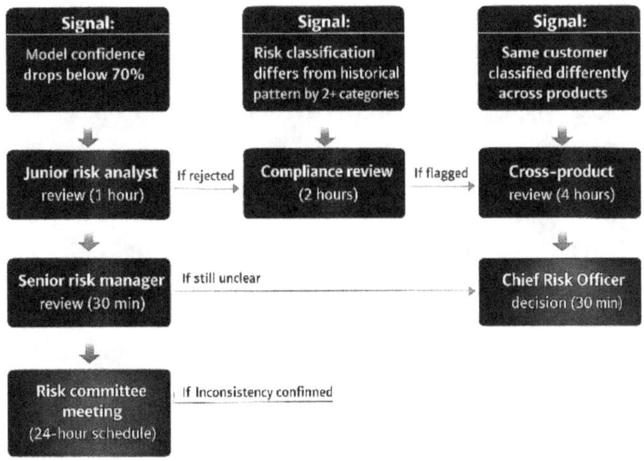

Each escalation has:

- Clear trigger (not "if something feels wrong")
- Clear owner
- Clear timeline
- Clear next decision

Play 4: Make Explainability a Leadership Obligation

The Problem:

Explainability is often treated as a technical feature.

In Phase II, it is a leadership responsibility.

If a leader cannot explain a decision, they should not have approved its automation.

The Play:

Before any AI system is deployed, the leader responsible must be able to explain:

1. What problem does this solve? (Clear business case)
2. How does it make decisions? (Intelligible to non-experts)
3. What are the key assumptions? (What could be wrong?)
4. When will it fail? (Boundary conditions)
5. Who is responsible if it goes wrong? (Explicit accountability)

If a leader cannot answer these clearly in writing, the system is not ready.

Real-World Example: GenAI in Loan Underwriting

INADEQUATE EXPLANATION:
"We use GenAI to assess loan applications. It generates underwriting summaries."

ADEQUATE EXPLANATION:
"GenAI system for loan underwriting:

- What it does: Analyzes credit history, income, debt, collateral; generates underwriting narrative

- How it decides: Trained on 50,000 historical loans; identifies risk drivers; generates explanation
- Key assumptions: Historical data is representative; risk drivers will persist
- Known limitations: Performance gaps for self-employed (10% of applications); recent immigrants (12%)
- When it fails: Confidence <60%; if customer profile outside training distribution; if market conditions change rapidly
- Override authority: Loan officer can override immediately without delay
- Accountability: VP Lending owns override policy; Chief Risk Officer owns model performance monitoring; Chief Compliance Officer owns regulatory alignment
- Explanation examples: [Include 5-10 real examples with original data and output]"

The leader must be able to write this.

If they cannot, they do not understand what they are deploying.

Play 5: Protect the Right to Challenge the Machine

The Problem:

As systems become more capable and confident, humans often stop challenging them.

This is called automation bias.

It is one of the most subtle and dangerous failures in Phase II.

The Play:

Explicitly protect and incentivize human challenge.

This means:

1. Document the right to disagree: Make it clear that disagreement with AI is expected, not discouraged.
2. Reduce friction for escalation: If someone wants to challenge a system decision, make it easy—not bureaucratic.
3. Reward good challenges: If someone surfaces a flaw the system missed, that should be recognized.
4. Investigate escalations seriously: When someone escalates a system decision, investigate why the system missed something.
5. Change policies accordingly: If challenges reveal systematic gaps, update the system's logic.

Real-World Example: Performance Rating System

DANGEROUS:

"HR AI generates performance ratings. Managers can override, but it's discouraged because 'the system is objective.'"

SAFE:

"HR AI generates performance ratings.

- Managers must review and sign off (cannot auto-approve)
- If manager disagrees, they escalate to HR Business Partner immediately (no delay)
- Any escalation triggers review of system's reasoning
- If >5% of escalations on the same issue → system logic is updated
- Managers who catch system biases are recognized in HR metrics"

The result: The system improves through feedback, and humans maintain agency.

Play 6: Align Responsibility with Control

The Problem:

This is where most Phase II leadership fails.

Humans are held responsible for outcomes they do not control.

"You are accountable for this AI's performance."
"But you won't let me override it."

This is organizational abuse.

The Play:

Simple rule: If you are responsible, you must have authority.

If a human is accountable for an outcome, they must have:

- Visibility into how the system decided
- Authority to override
- Real-time information to intervene
- Time to act (not seconds of notice after the fact)

Inversely: If you have no authority, you have no accountability.

If a system is fully autonomous, accountability belongs to those who designed it, not those who use it.

Real-World Example: Pricing Engine

MISALIGNED:
Regional manager is "accountable for margin."
System sets all prices autonomously.
Manager cannot override.
When prices are wrong → manager blamed.

ALIGNED:
Regional manager is "accountable for

margin."
System proposes prices (after analysis).
Manager reviews and approves daily.
System can override if real-time risk detected, but manager is notified within 5 minutes.
When prices are wrong → manager and system designers share accountability, based on who decided what.

Accountability follows authority.

Play 7: Redefine Performance for the AI Era

The Problem:

Traditional metrics reward output: volume, speed, efficiency.

In Phase II, these metrics incentivize the wrong behaviors.

A system that makes 1000 decisions fast but with low accountability is not performing well.
It is accumulating risk.

The Play:

Add new metrics that reward:

1. Quality of escalation: Did the system escalate appropriately?
2. Override accuracy: When humans overrode the system, were they right?

3. Audit cleanliness: Can decisions be explained?
4. Risk containment: Did exceptions catch problems before they scaled?
5. Stakeholder trust: Do humans trust the system? (Survey baseline)

Real-World Example: Compliance System

OLD METRICS:

- Transactions monitored per day
- False positive rate
- System uptime

NEW METRICS (ADDED):

- % of escalations that were justified (human review)
- Time from escalation to resolution
- Audit issues found in system-approved transactions
- Regulatory feedback on governance visibility
- Compliance team job satisfaction (Are they trusted to override?)

The new metrics incentivize accountability, not just throughput.

Play 8: Treat Governance as Strategy

The Problem:

Many leaders see governance as compliance burden.

In Phase II, governance is strategy.

How you govern AI determines:

- Whether regulators trust you
- Whether customers trust you
- Whether employees trust you
- Whether you can scale safely
- Whether you survive the first crisis

The Play:

Make governance visible, principled, and enforced.

This means:

1. Visible Governance: Make your decision rules, escalation logic, and accountability structures public (internally and externally when appropriate).
2. Principled Governance: Base governance on clear values, not ad-hoc decisions.
3. Consistent Enforcement: Apply governance fairly and consistently.

Real-World Example: Governance as Competitive Advantage

Company A: Deploys AI fast, governance is implied, explanations are vague.

Company B: Deploys AI methodically, governance is documented, explanations are clear.

Year 1: Company A pulls ahead (faster deployment).

Year 2: Both companies face regulatory inquiry.

- Company A struggles to explain decisions.
- Company B produces clear documentation.

Regulator requires both to slow down, but Company B's slowdown is briefer because governance was already in place.

Year 3: Company B recruits top talent more easily because employees trust the governance.

Year 5: Both companies deploy new systems.

- Company A has learned to govern (pain, slowdown).
- Company B continues at high speed with built-in governance.

Governance is not a cost.
It is a competitive advantage.

PART 3: IMPLEMENTATION SCENARIOS

Scenario 1: Financial Services - Portfolio Management

The Situation:

Large asset manager with $500B AUM wants to deploy quantum-assisted portfolio optimization.

Current state:

- Portfolio rebalancing takes 8 hours nightly
- Models optimize ~15,000 of 50,000 holdings
- Risk is approximate

Proposed state:

- Quantum optimization takes 2 hours
- Models optimize all 50,000 holdings
- Risk is more precise (but different assumptions)

The Leadership Challenge:

How do you deploy this safely? How do you govern it?

The Play-by-Play:

Step 1: Design Decision Boundaries

Who decides what?

DECISION BOUNDARY MATRIX

STRATEGIC DECISIONS (Board / CIO)	GOVERNANCE DECISIONS (CRO / Portfolio Committee)	OPERATIONAL DECISIONS (Portfolio Manager / System)
• Risk tolerance changes • Quantum pilot approval • Governance framework changes • Regulatory disclosure	• Model recalibration (if quantum changes behavior) • Escalation thresholds • Override triggers • Drift monitoring	• Daily rebalancing • Asset allocation • Risk adjustments • Trade execution

Step 2: Build Escalation Logic

When does the system stop and ask for help?

DECISION ESCALATION TRIGGERS

TRIGGER 1: Confidence Drop	TRIGGER 2: Risk Concentration	TRIGGER 3: Recommendation Differs from Historical Pattern	TRIGGER 4: Volatility Signal Spike
➡ **Signal:** • Model confidence <70%	➡ **Signal:** • Single holding >5% OR sector >30%	➡ **Signal:** • Quantum recommendation differs from classical by >10%	➡ **Signal:** • Market volatility >3 standard deviations
⇒ **Escalates to:** • Portfolio Committee	⇒ **Escalates to:** • CRO		⇒ **Escalates to:** • CIO
⇒ **Timeline:** • 30 minutes	⇒ **Timeline:** • 1 hour (or halt if >threshold)	⇒ **Timeline:** • 2 hours	⇒ **Timeline:** • Immediate (no rebalancing until cleared)
⇒ **Decision:** • Override or accept uncertainty	⇒ **Decision:** • Accept or reduce	⇒ **Decision:** • Test assumpion change • OR revert to hybrid approach	⇒ **Decision:** • Proceed, halt, or reduce quantum weighting

Step 3: Make Explainability Mandatory

Before deployment, CRO must write:

"Quantum portfolio optimization:

- What it does: Uses quantum algorithms to optimize risk-return across 50,000 holdings

- How it differs from classical: Can evaluate tail-risk scenarios that classical systems approximate
- Key assumptions: Quantum improvement is 15% (±5%); risk model changes will be detected; market structure remains stable
- When it fails: If quantum advantage degrades; if correlation assumptions break; if market regime shifts
- Boundaries: Sector limits remain; liquidity constraints apply; ESG screens apply
- Override authority: Portfolio managers can override any rebalancing recommendation (within risk limits)
- Monitoring: Daily drift analysis; weekly tail-risk comparison (quantum vs. classical); monthly governance review
- Examples: [Include 10 real portfolio scenarios with quantum vs. classical output]"

Step 4: Align Responsibility with Control

Who is accountable?

ACCOUNTABILITY MATRIX

SYSTEM PERFORMANCE	REGULATORY RELATIONSHIPS	TRADER EXPERIENCE	GOVERNANCE
→ Responsible: • Chief Data Officer	→ Responsible: • Chief Compliance Officer	→ Responsible: • Head of Trading	→ Responsible: • Board Audit Committee
⇒ Responsible: • Chief Data Officer	⇒ Authority: • Can override system recommendations; can halt trading if needed	⇒ Authority: • Can challenge system alerts; can request exceptions	⇒ Authority: • Can request system review; can require governance changes
⇒ Responsible: • Can tune detection sensitivity; can adjust confidence thresholds	⇒ Trader response: • Explain accuracy; false positive rate; audit trall quality	⇒ Accountability: • Regulatory reporting system governance; trader fairness	⇒ Accountability: • Trading profitability within guardrails; trust in compliance

If accountability is unclear, the system is not ready.

Step 5: Protect Override Rights

Make it clear:

"Portfolio managers can override any quantum recommendation. No approval needed. System will not delay. CRO reviews all overrides daily. If pattern emerges, we examine system logic. Managers who catch system biases are recognized."

Scenario 2: Regulatory Compliance - Real-Time Monitoring

The Situation:

Global bank wants to deploy real-time AI-driven market abuse detection across all trading desks.

Current state:

- Post-trade surveillance (reactive)
- 2-3 week investigation lag

- Manual rules, updated monthly

Desired state:

- Real-time monitoring (predictive)
- Immediate flagging
- AI learns patterns

The Leadership Challenge:

How do you flag traders in real-time without over-controlling? How do you preserve trust?

The Play-by-Play:

Step 1: Design Boundaries

What can the system decide?

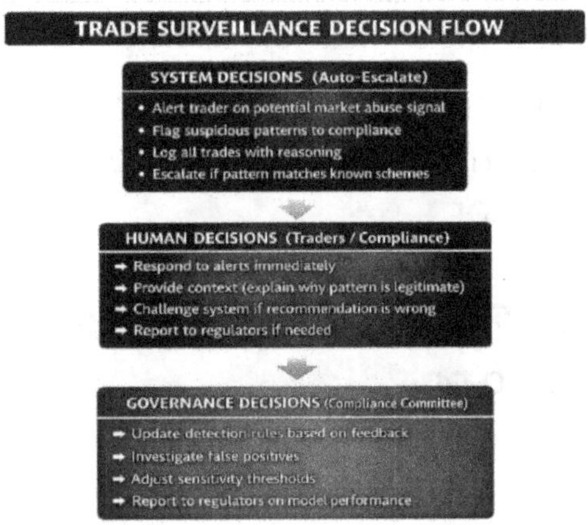

Step 2: Build Escalation Logic

When does detection trigger action?

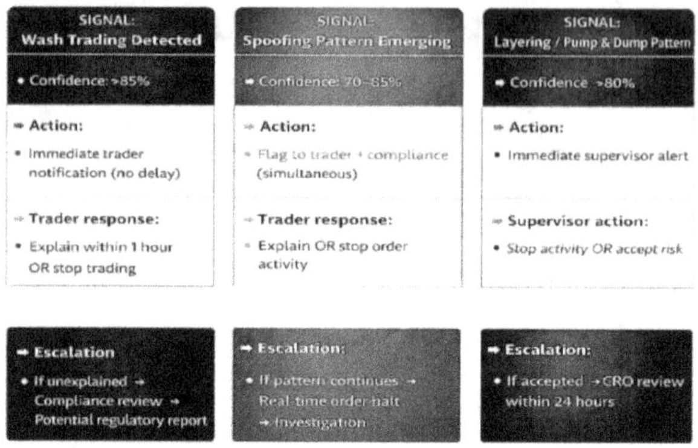

Step 3: Make Explainability Mandatory

Compliance Head must write:

"Real-time market abuse detection:

- What it monitors: Order timing, execution patterns, price movements, news correlation
- How it detects abuse: Flags patterns matching known schemes; alerts on unusual behavior
- Confidence thresholds: >85% = immediate action; 70-85% = escalation; <70% = logging only
- False positive rate: Historical 8% (acceptable); will improve with feedback
- Trader impact: Alerts are informational; traders can explain context; no automatic trading halts except >90% confidence
- Regulatory alignment: Detection rules reviewed by compliance; model updated monthly

- Transparency: Traders can see why they were flagged (within 24 hours)
- Examples: [Include 20 real scenarios with alert rationale, trader response, outcome]"

Step 4: Align Responsibility with Control

ACCOUNTABILITY MATRIX

SYSTEM PERFORMANCE	REGULATORY RELATIONSHIPS	TRADER EXPERIENCE	GOVERNANCE
→ Responsible: • Chief Data Officer	→ Responsible: • Chief Compliance Officer	→ Responsible: • Head of Trading	→ Responsible: • Board Audit Committee
⇒ Responsible: • Chief Data Officer	⇒ Authority: • Can override system recommendations; can halt trading if needed	⇒ Authority: • Can challenge system alerts; can request exceptions	⇒ Authority: • Can request system review; can require governance changes
⇒ Responsible: • Can tune detection sensitivity; can adjust confidence thresholds	⇒ Trader response: • Explain accuracy; false positive rate; audit trail quality	⇒ Accountability: • Regulatory reporting system governance; trader fairness	⇒ Accountability: • Trading profitability within guardrails; trust in compliance

Step 5: Protect Challenge Rights

Make it explicit:

"Traders can challenge market abuse alerts. Explain your position within 1 hour. Compliance reviews within 24 hours. If trader is right, system logic is updated. Traders who help improve detection are recognized in performance reviews. False alerts are not counted against trader performance metrics."

Scenario 3: Product Development - AI in Loan Underwriting

The Situation:

Regional bank wants to deploy AI-driven loan underwriting to speed approval from 5 days to 24 hours.

Current state:

- Manual underwriting by loan officers
- Consistent but slow
- Some subjective bias

Proposed state:

- AI analysis + human decision
- Fast screening + officer approval
- Potentially more consistent

The Leadership Challenge:

How do you preserve loan officer agency? How do you speed up without pushing responsibility onto humans?

The Play-by-Play:

Step 1: Design the Collaboration Model

Who decides what?

AI ROLE (Analysis)

- Analyze credit profile
- Identify risk drivers
- Generate underwriting narrative
- Recommend approve/decline/refer
- Flag for human review if uncertain

LOAN OFFICER ROLE (Decision)

- Review AI analysis and narrative
- Add context (relationship history, soft factors, market knowledge).
- Decide approve/decline/refer/escalate
- Take ownership of decision
- Overwrite AI if judgement dictates

MANAGEMENT ROLE (Governance)

- Monitor approval rates
- Audit officer decisions vs. AI recommendations
- Identify patterns or biases

Step 2: Build Escalation Logic

When does human judgment take over?

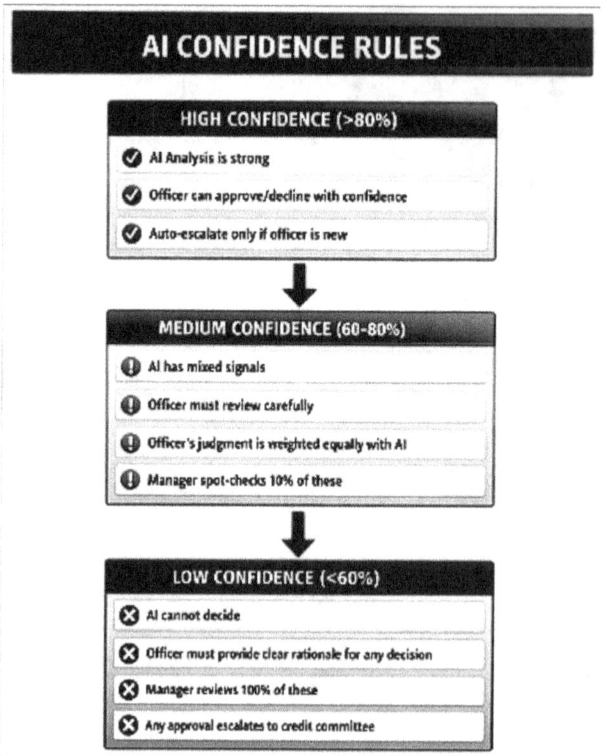

Step 3: Make Explainability Mandatory

Head of Lending must document:

"AI-Assisted Loan Underwriting:

- What it does: Analyzes income, credit, debt, collateral; generates underwriting summary; recommends decision
- How it decides: Trained on 10,000 historical loans; weights credit score (40%), debt-to-income (30%), employment stability (20%), collateral (10%)

- Confidence levels: >80% for clear cases; 60-80% for mixed signals; <60% for outliers
- Known biases: 15% higher approval rate for government-employed applicants (corrected in v2); 12% lower for self-employed (data gap, under review)
- Officer override: Unrestricted. Officers can approve or decline regardless of AI recommendation. Override rationale is logged.
- Fairness monitoring: Monthly review of approval rates by demographic; any >2% variance triggers investigation
- Performance tracking: Loan performance compared to AI prediction; system retrains quarterly if prediction accuracy drops >5%
- Transparency: Officers can explain AI reasoning to customers if asked
- Examples: [Include 30 real applications with AI reasoning, officer decision, loan outcome]"

Step 4: Align Responsibility with Control

ACCOUNTABILITY MATRIX

AI SYSTEM

Responsible: Credit Analytics Manager

Authority: Can retrain model; can adjust confidence thresholds; can add/remove factors

Accountability: Prediction accuracy; bias monitoring; audit trail quality

LOAN OFFICER DECISIONS

Responsible: Loan Officer

Authority: Can override AI; can escalate for human review

Accountability: Decision quality; portfolio performance; fairness in lending

CREDIT POLICY

Responsible: Chief Credit Officer

Authority: Can change underwriting rules; can pause AI for any reason

Accountability: Portfolio quality; regulatory compliance; discrimination prevention

GOVERNANCE

Responsible: Board Credit Committee

Authority: Can request model review; can require policy changes

Accountability: Ensuring fairness; protecting bank from adverse selection; customer trust

Step 5: Protect Officer Agency

Make it clear:

"Loan officers are empowered to make the final decision. AI is a tool, not a decision-maker. If you disagree with AI, explain your reasoning. All overrides are reviewed monthly. If patterns emerge in overrides, we improve the AI. Officers who catch AI errors are recognized. No officer will be punished for challenging the system if rationale is sound."

PART 4: BOARD-LEVEL GOVERNANCE

What Boards Must Ask (And How to Know If Leadership Has Answers)

Question 1: Do We Know Who Owns Each AI Decision?

Bad answer: "Our CTO owns AI governance."

Good answer:
"Every autonomous system has a documented owner.

- Marketing AI: VP Marketing (owns content quality, brand risks)
- Risk AI: CRO (owns financial risk, escalation authority)
- HR AI: CHRO (owns fairness, employee concerns)

- Compliance AI: Chief Compliance Officer (owns regulatory alignment) Each owner has documented authority to change, pause, or override the system."

Question 2: Can We Explain Our AI Decisions to a Regulator—in Writing?

Bad answer: "Our AI is accurate, so it should be fine."

Good answer:
"Yes. For each major AI system, we have documented:

- What it does and how it decides
- Who approves its deployment
- How it escalates when uncertain
- What overrides are available
- How we monitor for drift
- What we'll do if accuracy drops
- Examples of decisions and reasoning This documentation is updated quarterly and reviewed by external counsel."

Question 3: How Do We Know If Our AI Is Trustworthy?

Bad answer: "We measure accuracy metrics."

Good answer:
"We measure:

- Technical accuracy (yes)
- Stakeholder trust (survey: 70%+)

- Override accuracy (when humans override, they're right 65%+)
- Audit cleanliness (no unexplained decisions)
- Escalation quality (escalations are justified 80%+)
- Regulatory feedback (no concerns flagged)

All metrics reported monthly to board."

Question 4: If This AI Caused a Crisis Tomorrow, Could We Explain It Clearly?

Bad answer: "We have insurance."

Good answer:
"Yes. We could immediately provide:

- System architecture and decision logic
- Training data and validation results
- Escalation logs and override decisions
- Governance framework and approval chain
- Examples of good and bad decisions the system made
- Impact analysis (who was affected and how)

This documentation would support regulatory defense and customer communication."

Question 5: How Do We Prevent Automation Bias (Humans Blindly Trusting the System)?

Bad answer: "Our governance prevents that."

Good answer:
"We actively protect human override:

- Documenting right to challenge
- Reducing friction for escalation
- Reviewing all escalations seriously
- Updating system when humans catch errors
- Recognizing people who challenge the system

We monitor human override rates (should be 5-10%); if it drops below 2%, we investigate."

PART 5: FINAL PRINCIPLES

The Five Immutable Laws of AI Phase II Leadership

Law 1: Speed Without Accountability Is Recklessness

Faster decisions without governance structures is not progress.
It is systemic risk.

Move slowly where it matters.
Preserve authority where it is needed.

Law 2: Capability Without Credibility Is Fragility

A powerful system that cannot be explained will eventually fail—when trust is questioned.

Always design for explanation.

Law 3: Delegation Without Accountability Is Abandonment

If you assign someone responsibility for an AI decision without giving them authority to change it, you are setting them up to fail.

Responsibility and authority must align.

Law 4: Governance Is Strategy

Leadership that treats AI governance as a compliance checkbox will lose to leadership that treats it as competitive advantage.

Governance done well accelerates adoption.
Governance done poorly slows everything down—and still doesn't prevent crises.

Law 5: Humans Don't Compete With Machines—They Govern Them

The future is not human vs. machine.
It is human with machine—intentionally, carefully, responsibly.

Your job as leader is not to win that competition.
It is to design the collaboration.

BOARD BRIEFING VERSION

Why a Playbook — Not Another Theory

TEN SIGNALS – 2026-27: AI PHASE II

(Standalone Executive Report for Boards & CXOs)

EXECUTIVE SUMMARY

The Core Message:

By 2026-27, artificial intelligence enters Phase II—a phase where systems no longer assist humans, but increasingly act on their behalf. This shift is not theoretical. It is already visible in controlled deployments across finance, compliance, and operations.

The challenge ahead is not technological. It is governance.

This briefing is written for board members and senior executives navigating three critical questions:

1. What is actually changing? (Not hype—what signals are real?)
2. What does it mean for our organization? (Concrete implications)
3. What do we need to do? (Governance, not just adoption)

TEN SIGNALS AT A GLANCE

Signal	What's Changing	Why It Matters	Time line	Board Action
1. Agentic AI	Systems act autonomously, not just recommend	Accountability becomes critical	Q2-Q3 2026	Design decision rights
2. GenAI Maturity	Moves from content to decision support	Explainability becomes mandatory	Mid-2026	Require governance framework
3. GenAI Risk	Confidence without competence	Trust can evaporate quickly	Ongoing	Monitor automation bias
4. Embed	Financial decisions	Risk accumul	2026-27	Move governa

Signal	What's Changing	Why It Matters	Time line	Board Action
ded Finance	made invisibly	ates silently		nce to architecture
5. Privacy-Preserving AI	Data stays decentralized	Regulatory advantage to early movers	Q2-Q4 2026	Assess federated options
6. Quantum Computing	Selective advantage in optimization, cryptographic risk	Competitive and regulatory disadvantage to laggards	2026 - 2030	Inventory cryptography
7. RegTech Predictive	Compliance before rules change	6-12 month advantage to early movers	Q1-Q2 2026	Invest in regulatory intelligence
8. Credibility	Capability no longer enough	Trust becomes differentiator	2026 -27	Demand explainability

Signal	What's Changing	Why It Matters	Time line	Board Action
9. Human-Machine Collaboration	Humans don't compete—they govern	Collaboration by design	2026-27	Protect override rights
10. Phase II Verdict	Leadership is accountability, not speed	Maturity replaces automation	2026+	Center governance, not tools

SIGNAL 1: AGENTIC AI – FROM ASSIST TO ACT

What's Changing

Systems are beginning to initiate, sequence, and execute actions autonomously, without waiting for human approval on each step.

Concrete examples (currently deployed):

- Onboarding systems that auto-approve low-risk customers without human review
- Compliance systems that auto-escalate anomalies without waiting for analyst
- Reconciliation systems that execute corrections autonomously

- Risk systems that trigger hedges without explicit approval

Why It Matters for Boards

The governance shift:

When execution was human-controlled, accountability was clear: "The person who did it is responsible."

When systems act autonomously, accountability becomes: "Who designed the system to act this way?"

This is uncomfortable because it moves responsibility backward—to architects, designers, and approvers.

But it also clarifies it.

Board Risk (2026-27)

1. Regulatory gap: If your organization cannot clearly explain who has authority for system decisions, regulators will require you to tighten governance.
2. Escalation failure: If escalation logic is vague, it will fail under pressure (crisis, market stress, rare edge cases).
3. Talent risk: Employees become uncomfortable with AI autonomy when accountability is unclear.

Current Metrics (Q4 2025)

- Organizations with explicit decision-rights documentation: 42%
- Organizations without: 58%

- Regulatory inquiries about autonomous systems: +340% in 2025 (SEC, FCA, BaFin)

What Boards Should Require

By Q2 2026:

1. Decision-Rights Matrix: Document every major autonomous decision.

- Who initiates? (System / Human / Both)
- Who approves? (System / Human / Both)
- Who can override? (Explicit list)
- When does escalation trigger? (Explicit conditions)

2. Escalation Testing: Before deployment, test escalation logic.

- Can humans intervene when needed?
- Is the timeline realistic?
- Are responsibilities clear?

3. Accountability Assignment: For each system, one executive owns it.

- Document their authority
- Document what they can change
- Document what happens if they want to pause it

SIGNAL 2: GENERATIVE AI & THE SECOND MATURITY CURVE

What's Changing

GenAI is moving from content generation (writing, summarization) to decision support (explaining financials, simulating scenarios, drafting risk narratives).

This is less visible but far more consequential.

Why It Matters for Boards

The risk shift:

In Phase I, GenAI errors were visible: bad writing, obvious hallucinations. In Phase II, GenAI errors are subtle: plausible-sounding explanations that hide uncertainty.

A CFO reads: "Margin pressure is driven by raw material costs (42%), pricing delays (31%), and Plant B under-absorption (27%)."

The explanation sounds reasonable. The CFO believes it. No one questions the underlying assumptions.

If one of those assumptions is wrong, the organization acts on false premises.

Board Risk (2026-27)

1. Narrative capture: Organizations accept AI-generated explanations too easily, without questioning assumptions.
2. Hidden uncertainty: AI excels at sounding confident, even when confidence is low.

3. Governance failure: Organizations lack frameworks to validate AI-generated decisions.

Current Metrics (Q4 2025)

- Financial services firms using GenAI in decision support: 67%
- With governance frameworks: 31%
- Without frameworks: 69%
- Instances of "narrative capture" (over-reliance on AI explanation): 1 per 150 decisions

What Boards Should Require

By Q1 2026:

1. Explainability Mandate: Before GenAI is used in decisions, leadership must explain:

- What problem does it solve?
- How does it make decisions?
- What are the key assumptions?
- What's the confidence level?
- What are alternative interpretations?

2. Assumption Documentation: For every AI-generated narrative, document:

- Which data sources were used?
- What scenarios were considered?
- What was NOT included and why?
- What would need to change for this to be wrong?

3. Challenge Mechanisms: Ensure that leadership can:

- Ask "What else could explain this?"
- Demand alternative narratives
- Escalate uncertainty without penalty

SIGNAL 3: THE CONFIDENCE PROBLEM

What's Changing

As GenAI improves, its outputs sound increasingly certain—even when underlying confidence is low.

This creates a subtle but dangerous failure mode: automation bias. People stop questioning because explanations sound confident.

Why It Matters for Boards

This is where Phase II becomes genuinely risky.

Not because AI becomes less accurate, but because humans become more trusting.

Organizations fail not by deploying weak AI, but by deploying *strong* AI that people over-rely on.

Board Risk (2026-27)

1. Silent decision drift: Over time, humans default more to AI recommendations without challenging them.

2. Systemic exposure: Small, reasonable decisions compound into concentrated risk.
3. Crisis vulnerability: When the AI makes a wrong call, it might affect thousands of decisions before anyone notices.

Current Metrics (Q4 2025)

- GenAI false confidence (high certainty on low-confidence outputs): 12-18% of cases
- Regulatory actions citing over-reliance on AI explanation: 47 cases in US/EU (2025)
- Organizations that discovered automation bias post-failure: 34%

What Boards Should Require

By Q2 2026:

1. Confidence Transparency: Every AI output must come with:

- Confidence level (quantified)
- Uncertainty bounds
- Alternative interpretations
- Conditions under which it could be wrong

2. Human Override Culture: Explicitly protect and incentivize:

- The right to disagree with AI
- Easy escalation when uncertain

- Recognition for catching AI errors
- Investigation of automation bias

3. Monitoring for Drift: Track:

- % of AI recommendations accepted (should stay at 85-95%, not 98%+)
- % of human overrides that were correct
- Time to detect problems (should be <1 week, not months)

SIGNAL 4: EMBEDDED FINANCE BECOMES INVISIBLE

What's Changing

Financial decisions are being embedded directly into non-financial systems (apps, e-commerce platforms, workflows).

A customer clicks "buy now." Credit is extended. Pricing is adjusted. Compliance is checked. Risk is assumed.

All in 100 milliseconds. No human touches it.

Why It Matters for Boards

The visibility problem:

When finance was visible (invoices, approvals, reports), risk surfaced through:

- Delays
- Manual reviews

- Exceptions caught by human judgment

When finance is embedded, risk surfaces through:

- System design choices (coded logic)
- Data quality assumptions
- Escalation thresholds that might be too high
- Edge cases that no one predicted

Risk doesn't disappear. It moves into architecture.

Board Risk (2026-27)

1. Silent risk accumulation: Exposure builds without visibility until it's too late.
2. Design blind spots: Risk assumptions that are individually reasonable become dangerous collectively.
3. Crisis without warning: No manual review process to catch problems.

Current Metrics (Q4 2025)

- Embedded lending market: $35B (2025), projected $120B (2027)
- Incidents of silent risk accumulation: 16% of implementations
- Cost of post-deployment remediation: 3.4x higher than pre-deployment governance

What Boards Should Require

By Q2 2026:

1. Architecture Audits: For every embedded financial decision:

- Who designed it?
- What assumptions does it make?
- How is it monitored?
- Who can change it?
- How quickly can you intervene if it goes wrong?

2. Real-Time Monitoring: Don't wait for monthly reports.

- Daily risk concentration tracking
- Weekly tail-risk analysis
- Automated alerts when exposure hits thresholds
- Clear escalation to CRO

3. Governance in Design: Compliance cannot be bolted on later.

- Embedded decisions must have built-in controls
- Human override must be possible
- Escalation logic must be explicit

SIGNAL 5: PRIVACY-PRESERVING AI (FEDERATED LEARNING)

What's Changing

Organizations are shifting from central data warehouses to federated architectures where:

- Data stays decentralized
- Models train locally
- Only insights (not raw data) are shared

Why It Matters for Boards

Regulatory momentum is real:

- GDPR enforcement actions decreased 34% for privacy-by-design firms
- Data-localization rules are expanding across 12+ jurisdictions
- Regulators explicitly prefer federated architectures

Organizations moving early gain regulatory advantage. Those that delay face enforced retrofitting.

Board Risk (2026-27)

1. Regulatory disadvantage: Late movers face forced remediation (expensive, slow).
2. Data breach exposure: Centralized warehouses remain attractive targets.
3. Talent attraction: Employees worry about data practices; privacy-by-design is a signal of good governance.

Current Metrics (Q4 2025)

- Organizations with privacy-preserving AI pilots: 156 globally
- With complete crypto inventory: 18%

- With zero quantum-readiness plan: 70%

What Boards Should Require

By Q3 2026:

1. Privacy Architecture Audit:

- Where is personal data concentrated?
- Could it stay more decentralized?
- What's the regulatory advantage of federated learning?

2. Federated Learning Roadmap: For high-value use cases:

- Which models could train locally?
- What infrastructure is needed?
- What's the ROI (risk reduction + regulatory advantage)?

3. Data Minimization By Default: New AI projects should:

- Use only minimum necessary data
- Assume data localization rules
- Design for federated training from the start

SIGNAL 6: QUANTUM COMPUTING & SELECTIVE ADVANTAGE

What's Changing

Quantum computers excel at:

- Portfolio optimization (8+ hours → 2 hours)

- Risk modeling (quantum can evaluate tail scenarios classical systems approximate)
- Cryptographic factoring (RSA-2048 becomes vulnerable)

But they don't replace classical systems. They complement them selectively.

Why It Matters for Boards

Two distinct risks:

1. Cryptographic vulnerability: NIST deadline is 2026-2027 for post-quantum migration.
2. Competitive disadvantage: Institutions with quantum capability will demonstrate superior stress testing. Regulators will expect it from others.

Board Risk (2026-27)

1. Cryptographic migration failure: Historical encrypted data becomes readable in 2027-2030 if migration is not complete.
2. Regulatory disadvantage: Peers demonstrate deeper stress testing; you cannot.
3. Talent acquisition: Quantum-aware professionals are in high demand.

Current Metrics (Q4 2025)

- Organizations with quantum pilots: 187 globally; 34 in financial services

- HSBC optimization improvement: 34%
- JPMorgan pricing speed-up: 8.2x
- Organizations with complete crypto inventory: 18%
- With migration roadmaps: 12%

What Boards Should Require

By Q2 2026:

1. Cryptographic Inventory & Migration Plan:

- Where are RSA/ECC systems deployed?
- Which systems protect data that must remain secret for 10+ years?
- Migration timeline (should be 2026-2030)
- Cost estimate

2. Quantum Opportunity Assessment:

- Which optimization problems constrain performance today?
- Could quantum provide competitive advantage?
- What's the pilot cost vs. upside?

3. Quantum Literacy:

- Ensure risk/portfolio teams understand quantum implications
- Build relationships with quantum vendors/researchers
- Plan for quantum-native hiring

SIGNAL 7: REGTECH BECOMES PREDICTIVE

What's Changing

RegTech evolves
from reactive (checking today's rules) to predictive (anticipating tomorrow's rules and pre-complying).

Organizations that invest in regulatory intelligence gain 6-12 months of lead time on new rules.

Why It Matters for Boards

Competitive advantage AND regulatory standing:

- Institutions with predictive RegTech are compliant on day-one of new rules
- Regulators view them favorably (demonstrate governance maturity)
- 6-month advantage in product launches under new rules = significant revenue upside

Board Risk (2026-27)

1. Compliance lag: Reactors spend 3-6 weeks catching up after each rule change.
2. Regulatory attention: Reactive compliance invites more scrutiny.
3. Market opportunity loss: Predictors launch products faster under new rules.

Current Metrics (Q4 2025)

- Organizations with regulatory intelligence layers: 23 globally
- FCA rule-violation prediction accuracy: 94%
- Time advantage (predictive vs. reactive): 6-12 months
- Regulatory cost differential: 60% fewer enforcement inquiries for predictive firms

What Boards Should Require

By Q1 2026:

1. Regulatory Intelligence Layer:

- AI system that monitors regulatory signals (filings, speeches, consultations)
- Predicts likely rule changes 6-12 months in advance
- Flags implications for your business
- Cost: $5-10M annually; ROI: 6-month competitive advantage

2. Pre-Compliance Design: Before any product launch:

- Assess likely regulatory changes in next 18 months
- Design systems that already comply
- Reduce compliance rework from 20% to 2% of dev time

3. Policy-as-Code: Compliance rules should be:

- Coded, not documented
- Testable before deployment
- Rapidly updateable when rules change
- Auditable for regulatory review

SIGNAL 8: CREDIBILITY – CAPABILITY IS NO LONGER ENOUGH

What's Changing

Organizations discover that capability alone does not guarantee trust.

A powerful system that cannot be explained will eventually fail when trust is questioned.

Why It Matters for Boards

By 2026-27, credibility becomes the differentiator.

Capability is assumed (everyone has good models).
Credibility is earned (through governance, transparency, explainability).

Board Risk (2026-27)

1. Trust collapse: Even one unexplainable decision can erode confidence in entire systems.
2. Regulatory action: Explainability is now required by regulators in 12+ jurisdictions.

3. Talent and customer risk: Employees and customers avoid organizations with opaque AI.

Current Metrics (Q4 2025)

- Organizations experiencing credibility failure (deployment halted): 31%
- Stakeholder confidence (Capability alone): 34%
- Stakeholder confidence (Capability + Governance + Explainability): 89%

What Boards Should Require

By Q2 2026:

1. Explainability Mandate: Every AI system must come with:

- Clear documentation of how it decides
- Transparent assumptions and trade-offs
- Examples of good and bad decisions
- Audit trail showing reasoning

2. Credibility Metrics: Track:

- Stakeholder confidence (quarterly survey)
- Override accuracy (when humans disagree, are they right?)
- Audit cleanliness (can decisions be explained?)
- Regulatory feedback

3. Credibility Testing: Before deployment, leadership must be able to explain:

- What problem does this solve?
- How does it make decisions?
- What are the key assumptions?
- When will it fail?
- Who is responsible if it goes wrong?

SIGNAL 9: HUMAN-MACHINE COLLABORATION

What's Changing

The future is not human vs. machine. It is human with machine—intentionally designed collaboration.

Poor collaboration creates blind trust and automation bias.
Good collaboration creates resilient, intelligent systems.

Why It Matters for Boards

The accountability shift:

If humans are held responsible for AI outcomes, they must have:

- Authority to override
- Visibility into decisions
- Time to intervene
- Right to challenge

Misaligned responsibility = organizational failure.

Board Risk (2026-27)

1. Automation bias: Humans trust systems too much, stop questioning.
2. Accountability collapse: Humans blamed for outcomes they don't control.
3. Talent loss: Employees leave when agency is removed.

Current Metrics (Q4 2025)

- Organizations with documented override rights: 42%
- With explicit challenge encouragement: 18%
- With misaligned responsibility/control: 60%

What Boards Should Require

By Q2 2026:

1. Collaboration Design: For every AI system:

- What is human role? (Not rubber stamp)
- What is system role?
- Where do they interact?
- When can humans override?
- Is override frictionless?

2. Override Protection: Explicitly protect:

- Right to disagree with AI
- Frictionless escalation
- Investigation of challenges
- Recognition for catching errors

3. Responsibility Alignment: Never hold someone accountable without giving them authority.

- If a human is responsible, they can override
- If a system is responsible, humans are not blamed for its failure
- Accountability traces clearly

SIGNAL 10: THE PHASE II VERDICT

The Core Message

Technology will scale. Only maturity will differentiate.

By 2026-27, the organizations that thrive will be those that:

- Govern AI proactively (not reactively)
- Treat governance as strategy (not compliance)
- Protect human judgment (not replace it)
- Build credibility (not just capability)

What This Means for Boards

Five immutable truths:

1. Speed without accountability is recklessness. Move slowly where it matters.
2. Capability without credibility is fragility. Always design for explanation.

3. Delegation without authority is abandonment. Align responsibility with control.
4. Governance is strategy. Leadership that treats governance as a checkbox loses to leadership that treats it as competitive advantage.
5. Humans don't compete with machines. They govern them. Your job is to design the collaboration.

TIMELINE & DECISION GATES

Q1 2026

- Decision-rights documentation for all autonomous systems
- Explainability framework for GenAI deployments
- Cryptographic inventory complete
- Regulatory intelligence capabilities under review

Q2 2026

- Governance frameworks in place (Agentic, GenAI, Embedded Finance)
- Override mechanisms tested and documented
- Regulatory intelligence layer operational
- Privacy architecture audit complete

Q3 2026

- Federated learning pilots launched (where applicable)
- Quantum post-quantum cryptography migration roadmap finalized
- RegTech 3.0 deployment underway
- Credibility metrics tracking

Q4 2026

- All governance frameworks operational and audited
- Board confidence level: Can we explain every major AI decision? (Target: 100%)
- Competitive advantage visible in predictive compliance
- Quantum pilots showing ROI

KEY BOARD QUESTIONS

1. Governance Readiness

- Can we clearly explain who has authority for each AI decision?
- Do we have documented escalation logic for autonomous systems?
- Is responsibility aligned with control?

2. Trust & Credibility

- Can we defend our AI decisions to a regulator in writing?
- Do stakeholders trust our AI systems? (What does the data show?)

- What would it take to explain an AI failure publicly?

3. Regulatory Advantage

- Are we reactive or predictive in compliance?
- What regulatory changes could force system redesign? (In next 18 months)
- Are competitors building predictive compliance?

4. Risk & Resilience

- Where is financial risk embedded invisibly?
- Do we know what data we have and why?
- How quickly could we intervene if an AI system fails?

5. Talent & Culture

- Do employees trust our AI governance?
- Can they challenge systems without penalty?
- Are we attracting or losing talent to AI-mature competitors?

IMMEDIATE ACTIONS (NEXT 30 DAYS)

1. Assign Accountability: One executive per major AI system (owns governance, not just deployment)

2. Schedule Governance Audits: For each autonomous system:

- Who designed it?
- Can it be explained?
- Is escalation logic tested?
- Is accountability clear?

3. Establish Board Oversight: Add AI governance to board agenda

- Monthly: New deployments reviewed
- Quarterly: Governance health check
- Annually: Risk assessment

4. Benchmark Against Peers: Where are you relative to competitors?

- Governance maturity
- Regulatory readiness
- Credibility with stakeholders

CLOSING: THE REAL CHALLENGE

The challenge of AI Phase II is not technological.
It is governance.

The question is not: "How do we deploy AI faster?"

The question is: "How do we deploy AI responsibly—and build trust while doing it?"

Organizations that answer this clearly will lead.

Those that chase speed without maturity will struggle.

The signals are clear. The choices are yours.

About the Author

Jayant Gandhi is a strategic advisor, educator, and author with over three decades of experience spanning finance, risk, governance, technology-led transformation, and professional education. His work sits at the intersection of **emerging technologies and human judgment**, with a consistent focus on responsibility, decision-making, and long-term leadership maturity.

Across his career, Jayant has worked closely with students, mid-career professionals, CXOs, and boards navigating periods of structural change. He has seen how technologies reshape roles, how institutions respond under pressure, and how individuals either adapt thoughtfully—or struggle—when pace overtakes understanding. These experiences have shaped his belief that while capability evolves rapidly, **maturity must be cultivated deliberately**.

He is the author of ***Present and Future Technologies in Finance (PaFTiF),*** a practitioner-led work that examines the technological foundations transforming modern finance, including artificial intelligence, analytics, automation, blockchain, digital governance, and emerging regulatory frameworks. *PaFTiF* is widely used by students and professionals seeking clarity on how these technologies operate within real-world finance, risk, audit, and governance contexts.

While *PaFTiF* focuses on explaining **how systems work**, *Ten Signals – 2026–27* reflects Jayant's broader concern with **what those systems**

change—and who must take responsibility for their consequences. Together, the two books represent complementary perspectives: one technical and explanatory, the other reflective and leadership-oriented.

Jayant is Director – Strategy at **iBAS Global**, where he works on global professional education pathways and institutional collaborations, and mentors learners preparing for careers in an AI-mature world. He is known for encouraging learners and leaders alike to move beyond tools and credentials, toward judgment, accountability, and continuous learning. Contact: connect@jayantgandhi.com

At the core of his work lies a simple conviction:
technology will continue to evolve, but leadership is ultimately, defined by how one responds to change—with clarity, humility, and responsibility.

Website: Home - Jayant Gandhi – Author & Strategic Thought Leader

Note on Present and Future Technologies in Finance (PaFTiF)

Some readers may wish to explore the **technological foundations** that sit beneath many of the signals discussed in this book.

Present and Future Technologies in Finance (PaFTiF) was written for that purpose.

While *Ten Signals – 2026–27* focuses on **implications, maturity, and leadership judgment**, *PaFTiF* examines the **underlying technologies** shaping modern finance and enterprise decision-making. It covers themes such as artificial intelligence, analytics, automation, blockchain, digital governance, emerging regulatory frameworks, and the evolving role of finance professionals in technology-enabled organisations.

The intent of *PaFTiF* is explanatory rather than prescriptive. It seeks to demystify technologies that are often discussed in fragments, and to place them within real-world finance, risk, audit, and governance contexts.

The two books are designed to be **complementary**, not sequential.

- *PaFTiF* helps readers understand **how systems work**
- *Ten Signals – 2026–27* helps readers reflect on **what those systems change—and who must take responsibility for their consequences**

Each can be read independently. Together, they offer a fuller perspective for those navigating an AI-mature professional landscape.

Those interested may note that *Present and Future Technologies in Finance (PaFTiF)* is available on Amazon, with a dedicated India edition accessible at: https://u.payu.in/PAYUMN/Pr2299HhfXgY

Final Word: Change Is the Only Constant

Change is not new.

What is new is the **speed at which it now arrives**, the **scale at which it operates**, and the **distance between decision and consequence**. What once unfolded gradually now compounds. What once allowed correction now demands foresight.

I have lived long enough to know that change does not ask for permission.
It arrives—quietly or violently—and then asks a far more difficult question: *how will you respond?*

In business, in technology, and in life, I have seen one pattern repeat itself relentlessly. Tools change. Titles change. Institutions change. What endures is not competence alone, but **character under pressure**.

Artificial intelligence accelerates this truth.
It does not create human weakness or strength—it **amplifies** them.

Where there is clarity, it scales clarity. Where there is confusion, it scales

confusion.
Where there is responsibility, it multiplies impact.
Where there is avoidance, it multiplies risk.

This is why the future will not be decided by intelligence alone.

It will be decided by **judgment**.

What Experience Eventually Teaches

Early in our journeys, we chase certainty.
Later, we realise certainty is rare—and often misleading.

What matters more is the ability to:

- pause when others rush
- question when others comply
- learn when others defend
- take responsibility when others explain

I have learned, sometimes painfully, that success without self-awareness is fragile, and speed without wisdom is dangerous. The day one stops learning, one begins to decline—no matter how impressive the résumé or how advanced the tools.

Change humbles everyone eventually.
The wise allow it to teach them earlier.

Technology Will Not Save Us From Ourselves

There is a comforting myth that smarter systems will compensate for human limitations. That automation will reduce error. That intelligence will remove bias. That speed will produce better outcomes.

Reality is less forgiving.

Systems reflect the values, assumptions, and incentives of those who design and deploy them. When judgment is absent, technology does not correct it—it **hides it**. When accountability is unclear, technology does not resolve it—it **diffuses it**.

This is why maturity matters more than adoption.

Progress is not defined by how quickly we deploy what is possible, but by how responsibly we decide **what should be done, and what should not**.

A Personal Truth

Life has taught me that growth is rarely linear. Careers pause. Paths diverge. Convictions are tested. Sometimes the most important lessons arrive not through success, but through humility, failure, and reflection.

What kept me grounded was not certainty, but a few simple principles:

- stay curious

- keep learning
- own your choices
- treat people as ends, not means

These principles matter even more in an AI-mature world.

Because when systems act on our behalf, it is our values that act through them.

To the Reader

If there is one message, I hope you carry forward, it is this:

Change is inevitable.
Direction is a choice.

You do not need to outrun change.
You need to **understand it early, respond thoughtfully, and act responsibly**.

The signals are already visible.
The future is not waiting.

What remains is leadership—in careers, in organisations, and in life.

Change is the only constant.
Responsibility is the only stabiliser.

— *Jayant Gandhi,* Home - Jayant Gandhi – Author & Strategic Thought Leader

APPENDIX A: GLOSSARY

Key Terms and Definitions

A

Agentic AI
Systems that independently initiate, sequence, and execute actions across multi-step workflows without waiting for human approval on each step. Unlike assistive AI (which recommends), agentic systems act autonomously within predefined boundaries. Example: An onboarding system that auto-approves low-risk customer applications without manual review.

Algorithmic Trading
Automated execution of trades based on pre-programmed decision rules. Systems analyze market conditions, execute orders at optimal timing, and manage positions without human intervention. Creates both efficiency gains and systemic risk if governance is weak.

Anomaly Detection
AI technique that identifies unusual patterns or outliers in data. In compliance, flags suspicious transactions. In operations, signals equipment failures. Requires

threshold calibration to balance catch-rate (catching problems) vs. false positive rate (flagging legitimate activity).

Automation Bias
Cognitive tendency for humans to over-rely on automated suggestions and under-question them. As AI becomes more capable and confident, automation bias increases. Organizations fail not from weak AI, but from humans trusting strong AI too much.

B

Blockchain
Distributed ledger technology where transactions are grouped in blocks, cryptographically linked in a chain. Each participant maintains a copy. No central authority controls the ledger. Foundation for cryptocurrency and smart contracts.

Board Briefing Summary
A concise, one-page-per-signal executive summary designed for board-level review and decision-making. Translates technical signals into governance implications and required actions.

C

Centralized AI Architecture
Traditional approach: Data flows to central warehouse → Models train on pooled data → Systems deployed. Creates efficiency

but concentrates risk—a breach exposes all data at once.

Certification (Blockchain)
Verification and approval by authorized parties. In smart contracts, certification gates can trigger automated execution (e.g., "Insurance company certifies claim" → immediate payout).

Confidence Threshold
Minimum confidence level required for an AI system to act autonomously. Below threshold, system escalates to human. Example: "Auto-approve loans only if confidence >85%; otherwise escalate." Directly affects false positive rates and human workload.

Credibility
Trust earned through documented governance, transparent explainability, and consistent accountability. Different from confidence (which is statistical). An AI system can be highly confident but low credibility if it cannot explain its reasoning.

Cryptography / Cryptographic System
Mathematical technique to secure information so only intended recipients can read it. RSA-2048 and ECC are common systems. Vulnerable to quantum computers; NIST post-quantum algorithms are migration targets by 2026-2027.

D

Decentralized AI (Federated Learning)
Architecture where data remains at source (local institutions, devices), models train locally, and only insights/updates are shared. Privacy-preserving; aligns with GDPR and data-localization requirements.

Decision Intelligence
AI's role moving from content generation (creating outputs) to decision support (explaining variances, simulating scenarios, advising leaders). Phase II of AI maturity.

Decision Rights Matrix
Explicit documentation of who initiates, approves, can override, and is accountable for each decision type. Essential for autonomous AI systems. If unclear, governance fails under pressure.

Derivatives
Financial contracts whose value depends on underlying assets (stocks, bonds, commodities). Exotic derivatives are complex (non-standard); require sophisticated pricing models that benefit from quantum acceleration.

DeFi (Decentralized Finance)
Financial services (lending, trading, insurance) built on blockchain without traditional intermediaries. Relies on smart contracts and tokenization. Removes intermediaries; adds complexity and technical risk.

E

Embedded Finance
Financial decisions (credit, pricing, compliance) embedded directly into non-financial systems (apps, e-commerce, platforms). Invisible to users; risk accumulates silently. Governance must move to architecture level.

Escalation Logic
Explicit rules for when a system must hand off to humans. Example: "If confidence <70%, escalate to risk manager within 30 minutes." Critical for autonomous systems; if vague, fails under pressure.

EU AI Act
European Union regulation classifying AI systems as:

- Prohibited risk: Not allowed (e.g., real-time biometric ID)
- High-risk: Requires pre-deployment approval, documentation, monitoring
- Limited risk: Transparency requirements
- Minimal risk: No restrictions

Enforcement begins Q1 2026.

F

Fairness (AI)
Ensuring AI systems do not discriminate unfairly against individuals or groups. Measured by comparing approval rates, error rates across demographic groups.

Requires both technical and governance approaches.

Federated Learning
See Decentralized AI.

Financial Risk Modeling
Quantifying potential losses under various scenarios (market stress, credit defaults, liquidity shocks). Classical models use approximations (Gaussian distributions); quantum systems can evaluate fatter tails accurately.

FP&A (Financial Planning & Analysis)
Function responsible for forecasting, variance analysis, scenario modeling, capital planning. GenAI increasingly used for explanation and scenario simulation in Phase II.

G

Generative AI (GenAI)
AI systems trained on large datasets that generate new content (text, images, code). Phase I: Content generation. Phase II: Decision support (explanation, narrative generation, scenario simulation).

Governance
The framework for who decides what, who has authority, how escalation works, and who is accountable. In Phase II, governance is strategy (not compliance burden).

GDPR (General Data Protection Regulation)

European data protection law. Key principles: Data minimization, user consent, data localization, right to explanation. Drives privacy-by-design and federated learning adoption.

H

Hallucination (AI)
When AI generates confident but false information. Example: GenAI cites a journal article that doesn't exist. Less of a risk in Phase II (decision support) than Phase I; more dangerous is plausible hallucination (sounds true but assumptions are wrong).

Hybrid Quantum-Classical
System that divides work: Classical systems handle routine tasks; quantum handles optimization/simulation. Reduces infrastructure needs; leverages quantum advantage selectively.

I

Interoperability
Ability of different systems to work together, exchange data, and coordinate. In federated learning, interoperability between local models is critical. In blockchain, bridges allow different chains to interact.

J

Judgment
Human cognitive capacity to weigh competing considerations and decide when rules are ambiguous or edge cases emerge. Phase II emphasis: Judgment is what humans provide; execution is what AI provides.

K

KYC (Know Your Customer)
Regulatory requirement to verify customer identity, assess risk, monitor ongoing transactions. Increasingly automated through AI; governance must remain clear.

L

Latency
Delay between signal and response. Real-time systems must have low latency (<100ms). Critical in trading, fraud detection. Quantum-classical hybrid must manage latency carefully.

Liquidity
Ability to quickly buy/sell assets without moving prices significantly. Liquidity constraints limit portfolio optimization; real-time systems must respect them.

M

Machine Learning
AI technique where systems learn patterns from data without being explicitly

programmed. Underlies most AI systems in this book (agentic, GenAI, risk models). Requires training data quality and governance.

Margin
Profit remaining after costs. In trading, also refers to collateral required for derivatives positions. Embedded finance systems manage margin dynamically; requires tight governance.

Market Abuse
Illegal trading practices: spoofing (fake orders), layering (coordinated orders), wash trading (self-dealing), pump-and-dump (price manipulation). AI detects patterns in real-time.

Monte Carlo Simulation
Risk modeling technique that runs thousands of scenarios to estimate probability distributions. Classical systems are slow; quantum can evaluate same distribution 100x faster.

N

Narrative Capture
Risk where stakeholders over-accept AI-generated explanations without questioning assumptions. Phase II danger: AI explanations sound confident; humans stop asking "what else could explain this?"

NIST (National Institute of Standards & Technology)
US standards body. In context of this book,

NIST post-quantum cryptography standards (2024) define which algorithms replace RSA/ECC by 2026-2030.

O

Opaque AI / Black Box
AI systems where decision logic is not easily interpretable to humans. Deep neural networks are opaque; decision trees are transparent. Phase II requires moving toward explainability.

Override Rights
Authority to reject an AI decision and substitute human judgment. Essential for credibility; if users cannot override, trust erodes. Must be frictionless to be effective.

P

Phase II (AI Phase II)
Period (2026-27 onward) where AI systems move from assisting humans to acting autonomously. Core challenge shifts from capability to governance.

Policy-as-Code
Storing regulatory rules as executable code (not documents). Allows rapid testing, deployment, and auditing of compliance rules. Key enabler of predictive RegTech.

Post-Quantum Cryptography (PQC)
Cryptographic algorithms resistant to quantum attacks. NIST approved ML-KEM,

ML-DSA, SLH-DSA in 2024. Migration timeline: 2026-2030.

Predictive Compliance / Predictive RegTech
RegTech evolution where AI anticipates rule changes (6-12 months in advance) and pre-designs systems for compliance. Gives early movers 6-month competitive advantage.

Privacy-Preserving AI
AI architectures where data remains decentralized; insights are shared. Federated learning is primary example. Aligns with GDPR and emerging data-localization rules.

Q

Quantum Computing
Computing using quantum bits (qubits) that leverage superposition and entanglement for exponential speedup on specific problem classes. Selective advantage: Portfolio optimization, risk modeling, cryptography. Not universal acceleration.

Quantum Advantage
Performance improvement where quantum computers solve problems exponentially faster than classical systems. Example: RSA-2048 factoring (millions of years → hours).

R

Regulatory Intelligence
Monitoring regulatory environment (filings, speeches, consultations) using AI to predict likely rule changes before publication. Enables predictive compliance.

Regulatory Timeline
Schedule of when rules take effect. Board must track this for strategic planning. Example: EU AI Act high-risk compliance (April 2026), NIST PQC migration (2026-2030).

RegTech (Regulatory Technology)
Technology enabling compliance with regulations. Evolution: Reactive (check today's rules) → Predictive (anticipate tomorrow's rules).

Resilience
Ability to maintain operations under stress, recover from failures, adapt to changes. Phase II emphasis: Can your system survive when AI fails? Are escalation paths tested?

Risk Model Invalidation
Structural failure where classical approximations no longer hold when quantum capability arrives. Example: VaR models assume Gaussian distributions; quantum enables accurate fat-tail evaluation, revealing classical models underestimated risk.

RSA-2048
Common cryptographic algorithm protecting ~80% of encrypted systems. Vulnerable to quantum factoring. Migration to post-

quantum alternatives required by 2027-2030.

S

Scenario Simulation
Running "what-if" analyses to understand impact of hypothetical events. GenAI increasingly used to generate and explain scenarios; quantum can evaluate far more scenarios in same time.

Smart Contracts
Self-executing code on blockchains that automatically enforces agreements. Execute when conditions are met. No intermediary; creates efficiency and risk.

Spoofing
Market abuse where trader places large orders with no intention to execute, creating false impression of demand. AI detects through order pattern analysis.

Stress Testing
Risk management practice: Model portfolio behavior under extreme scenarios. Regulators require it. Quantum enables deeper stress testing (evaluating more scenarios accurately).

T

Tail Risk
Risk of extreme events (more extreme than normal distributions suggest). Fat-tailed distributions have higher tail risk. Quantum

can evaluate tail risk accurately; classical models approximate.

Tokenization
Converting real-world assets or future cash flows into digital tokens on blockchain. Creates liquidity and programmability. Foundation for DeFi.

Trust
Stakeholder confidence that system will behave as intended, be explainable when needed, and be governed responsibly. Earned through credibility (governance + explainability + accountability), not just capability.

U

Uncertainty Quantification
Explicitly estimating confidence levels and ranges in predictions. Phase II requirement: Every AI output must include confidence bounds, not just point estimates.

V

VaR (Value at Risk)
Risk metric: Expected maximum loss at given confidence level (e.g., 95% VaR = worst 5% of scenarios). Classical VaR uses Gaussian approximation; quantum enables accurate evaluation.

W

Wash Trading
Market abuse where trader buys and sells same security to themselves, creating false impression of volume. AI detects through transaction pattern analysis.

X-Z

Zero-Trust Architecture
Security approach: Verify every access request, assume breach is possible. In AI governance, similar approach: Verify every decision, assume bias/error is possible. Requires escalation and monitoring.

APPENDIX B: BOARD BRIEFING SUMMARY

1-Page Per Signal (Board Discussion Ready)

SIGNAL 1: AGENTIC AI – FROM ASSIST TO ACT

The Core Issue

Systems are beginning to execute autonomously, without waiting for human approval on each step. When humans made all decisions, accountability was clear. When systems act autonomously, accountability becomes: "Who designed the system to decide this way?"

What's at Stake

- Governance gap: 58% of organizations lack explicit decision-rights documentation for autonomous systems
- Regulatory pressure: SEC, FCA, BaFin issued 340% more inquiries about AI autonomy in 2025

- Escalation failure: If escalation logic is vague, it fails when problems emerge

Board Question
Can we document, for every major autonomous system:

1. Who initiates the decision?
2. Who approves it?
3. Who can override it?
4. When does escalation trigger?
5. Who owns the outcome if something goes wrong?

If Yes: Governance is proactive. Proceed with cautious scaling.

If No: Pause autonomous expansion. Create decision-rights matrix before new deployments.

Action Required (Q1 2026)
Document decision rights for top 10 autonomous systems. One executive per system owns governance.

SIGNAL 2: GENERATIVE AI & SECOND MATURITY CURVE

The Core Issue
GenAI is moving from content generation (writing, summarization) to decision support (explaining financials, simulating scenarios). This is less visible but far more consequential.

What's at Stake

- Narrative capture: 67% of financial services use GenAI in decisions; only 31% have governance frameworks
- Hidden uncertainty: GenAI excels at sounding confident, even when confidence is low
- Assumption transparency: Organizations accept explanations without questioning underlying assumptions

Board Question
For any AI-generated explanation influencing decisions, can leadership clearly state:

1. What sources does it use?
2. What are the key assumptions?
3. What would need to be true/false for this to be wrong?
4. What alternative interpretations exist?
5. What's the confidence level (quantified)?

If Yes: Governance exists. Monitor for drift.

If No: Require explainability mandate. No decision-critical GenAI use without documented assumptions.

Action Required (Q1 2026)
Implement explainability framework for all GenAI systems in decision support.

SIGNAL 3: THE CONFIDENCE PROBLEM

The Core Issue

As GenAI improves, humans trust it more—even when uncertainty remains. This creates automation bias: people stop questioning confident-sounding answers.

What's at Stake

- Silent decision drift: Over time, humans escalate less to AI recommendations
- Systemic risk: Small, reasonable decisions compound into concentrated exposure
- Crisis vulnerability: When AI makes a wrong call, thousands of decisions may be affected before anyone notices

Board Question

1. What % of AI recommendations are accepted without human challenge? (Should be 85-95%, not 98%+)
2. When humans override AI, are they right? (If >90%, humans are rubber-stamping)
3. How quickly would we detect an AI system making systematic errors? (Should be <1 week)

If these metrics are healthy: Trust is balanced. Continue.

If they're unhealthy: Automation bias exists. Redesign override mechanisms.

Action Required (Q2 2026)
Establish dashboard tracking:

- % of AI recommendations accepted
- % of overrides that were correct
- Time to detect systematic errors

SIGNAL 4: EMBEDDED FINANCE BECOMES INVISIBLE

The Core Issue
Financial decisions are embedded directly into non-financial systems (apps, e-commerce, workflows). Credit is extended, pricing adjusted, compliance checked—all invisibly, in milliseconds.

What's at Stake

- Silent risk: Risk accumulates without visibility until crisis
- Design blind spots: Reasonable risk assumptions become dangerous collectively
- No warning: Unlike manual processes, no human review to catch problems

Board Question
For each embedded financial decision, can we answer:

1. What assumptions does the system make about risk?

2. How is exposure monitored daily (not monthly)?
3. Who can intervene if risk concentrates?
4. How quickly can governance be changed?

If answers are clear: Architecture-level governance exists.

If vague: Risk is hidden. Require daily monitoring and escalation paths.

Action Required (Q2 2026)
Audit all embedded finance systems. Implement real-time risk concentration monitoring.

SIGNAL 5: PRIVACY-PRESERVING AI

The Core Issue
Data is centralizing (warehouse model); regulations are decentralizing (localization, minimization rules). Federated learning breaks this tension by letting data stay local while insights flow.

What's at Stake

- Regulatory timing: GDPR enforcement actions decreased 34% for privacy-by-design firms
- Data breach exposure: Centralized warehouses remain attractive targets

- Talent attraction: Privacy-conscious culture is competitive advantage

Board Question

1. Where is personal data concentrated (in central warehouse)?
2. Could federated learning reduce that concentration?
3. What's the regulatory advantage of early adoption?
4. What's the cost-benefit?

If federation is viable: Consider 2026-2027 pilot.

If not: Ensure data minimization is default; plan distributed architecture longer-term.

Action Required (Q3 2026)
Privacy architecture audit. Evaluate federated learning for 2-3 high-value use cases.

SIGNAL 6: QUANTUM COMPUTING & SELECTIVE ADVANTAGE

The Core Issue
Quantum offers:

1. Opportunity: Portfolio optimization (8 hrs → 2 hrs), deeper risk modeling
2. Risk: RSA-2048 cryptography becomes vulnerable in 2027-2030

What's at Stake

- Cryptographic deadline: NIST migration must complete by 2026-2030
- Historical data: Encrypted data can be decrypted later if not migrated
- Competitive disadvantage: Peers with quantum demonstrate superior stress testing; regulators will expect it

Board Question

1. What's our cryptographic inventory? (18% of orgs have complete inventory; 70% have zero plan)
2. Which encrypted data must remain secret beyond 2030?
3. What's our migration timeline?
4. Do we have a quantum opportunity assessment?

If plan exists: On track.

If not: Create cryptographic inventory and migration roadmap (Q1 2026).

Action Required (Q2 2026)
Complete crypto inventory and post-quantum migration roadmap.

SIGNAL 7: REGTECH BECOMES PREDICTIVE

The Core Issue
RegTech evolves
from reactive (checking today's rules)

to predictive (anticipating tomorrow's rules and pre-complying).

What's at Stake

- 6-12 month advantage: Predictive firms are compliant on day-one of new rules; reactive firms spend 3-6 weeks catching up
- Regulatory standing: Early adopters are viewed favorably by regulators
- Market opportunity: 6-month lead in product launches under new rules = significant revenue upside

Board Question

1. Are we reactive or predictive in compliance?
2. Do we monitor regulatory signals (filings, speeches, consultations)?
3. Can we anticipate rule changes and pre-design systems?
4. What's the competitive advantage of early adoption?

If predictive infrastructure exists: Competitive advantage building.

If reactive only: Invest in regulatory intelligence layer (ROI: 6-month lead time).

Action Required (Q1 2026)
Establish regulatory intelligence

capability. Target 6-12 month prediction horizon.

SIGNAL 8: CREDIBILITY – CAPABILITY IS NO LONGER ENOUGH

The Core Issue

Capability (power, accuracy) is assumed. Credibility (explainability, governance, trustworthiness) is earned.

What's at Stake

- Trust collapse: One unexplainable decision can erode confidence in entire systems
- Regulatory requirement: Explainability now required by regulators in 12+ jurisdictions
- Talent/customer risk: Employees and customers avoid organizations with opaque AI

Board Question

1. Can we explain every major AI decision in writing to a regulator?
2. Do stakeholders trust our AI? (Measure: Survey, shows 89% confidence with governance + explainability vs. 34% with capability alone)
3. If an AI failure occurred, could we defend our governance publicly?

If yes to all: Credibility is strong. Monitor.

If no: Implement explainability mandate and governance documentation.

Action Required (Q2 2026)
Establish credibility metrics (trust surveys, explainability docs, audit cleanliness).

SIGNAL 9: HUMAN-MACHINE COLLABORATION

The Core Issue
The future is not human vs. machine. It's human with machine—where humans govern, systems execute.

What's at Stake

- Automation bias: Humans over-trust systems, stop questioning
- Accountability collapse: Humans blamed for outcomes they don't control
- Talent loss: Employees leave when agency is removed

Board Question

1. For each major AI system, do humans have clear override rights?
2. Is escalation frictionless? (No bureaucracy preventing challenge)
3. When humans challenge the system, does leadership investigate seriously?

4. Are people recognized for catching AI errors?

   If all yes: Healthy collaboration.

   If no: Redesign for human agency. Protect override rights explicitly.

   Action Required (Q2 2026)
   Document override mechanisms. Protect and incentivize human challenge.

SIGNAL 10: THE PHASE II VERDICT

The Core Message
Technology will scale. Only maturity will differentiate.

The Five Immutable Laws

1. Speed without accountability = recklessness
2. Capability without credibility = fragility
3. Delegation without authority = abandonment
4. Governance = strategy (not compliance)
5. Humans don't compete with machines—they govern them

What's at Stake

- Leadership differentiation: Mature governance = competitive advantage
- Regulatory positioning: Early maturity = favorable regulatory standing

- Talent attraction: Governance-mature organizations attract top talent
- Crisis resilience: Mature organizations recover faster from AI failures

Board Question
Can we say with confidence: "We govern AI proactively, not reactively"?

If yes: You're ahead of 70% of competitors.
If no: This is your competitive disadvantage.

Action Required (Now)
Make AI governance visible, documented, and monitored. Treat it as strategic priority (not compliance checkbox).

www.ingramcontent.com/pod-product-compliance
Lightning Source LLC
Chambersburg PA
CBHW062134160726
48282CB00027B/824
* 9 7 8 9 3 5 6 3 5 2 8 7 2 *